S U R F
C A F É
L I V I N G

RECIPES, TIPS AND IDEAS INSPIRED BY THE OCEAN FROM THE AUTHORS OF THE SURF CAFÉ COOKBOOK

By **Jane** and **Myles Lamberth**

SURF CAFÉ LIVING

COOKING, ENTERTAINING AND LIVING BY THE SEA

Jane and Myles Lamberth
With Shannon Denny

Published by Orca Publications

EDITOR: Louise Searle
COPY EDITOR: Shannon Denny
PHOTOGRAPHER: Mike Searle
DESIGNER: David Alcock
ASSISTANT DESIGNER: Jamin Lean
ILLUSTRATIONS: Paula Mills, David Alcock
DISTRIBUTION: Chris Power
PROOF READER: Hayley Spurway

PHOTOGRAPHIC CONTRIBUTORS: Mark Capitallan, Mickey Smith, Christian McLeod, Andrew Kilfeather

Photographs on pages: 4, 16, 22, 23, 24, 26, 28, 36, 37, 49, 54, 55, 60, 61, 62, 65, 80, 100, 103, 106, 107, 116, 117, 126, 127, 128, 141, 148, 168, 172, 173 © Mark Capilitan; 59 © Christian McLeod; 32, 59, 185, 186, 191 © Andrew Kilfeather; 146 © Mickey Smith
Illustrations on pages: 41 © Nicola Colton

Surf Café Living ISBN 978-0-9567893-6-5

PRINTED AND BOUND: Great Wall Printing, Hong Kong
Published by Orca Publications
Berry Road Studios, Berry Road, Newquay, Cornwall, TR7 1AT, United Kingdom
TEL: (+44) 01637 878074 **FAX:** (+44) 01637 850226 **WEB:** www.orcasurf.co.uk

WWW.THESURFCAFECOOKBOOK.COM

CONTENTS

Welcome again.

So many exciting things have happened to myself and Myles since we brought out our last book, the Surf Café Cookbook. We opened our cool Little Shop next door to Shells Café, selling amazing artisan food, and we got a dog called Milkshake who is known throughout the village. And one of our most exciting adventures was creating our dream home.

A year ago Myles and I spotted a 100 year-old cottage with a back garden overlooked by a beautiful mountain. It was rundown, damp and empty. It was exactly what we were looking for, somewhere we could put our own stamp. Little did we know it, but spotting this little cottage was the start of our next journey - creating a home, a heart and an open house for friends and family.

In a year, with a lot of hard work and vision, we've turned the shell of a house into a beautiful dream home, which has allowed us to embrace our creative passions, as well as indulge our lifestyle of surf, the sea and hosting. Food is a big part of entertaining in our house, whether it's for a special event, lunch with a friend or roasting marshmallows over the fire. Whatever the occasion we like to make the tastiest food we can.

In Surf Café Living we'd like to show you how easy it is to create good home cooking using fresh, simple, local ingredients - food that's not complicated or pretentious but tasty, healthy and readily available. We'll take you on our journey of transforming a rundown, leaky house and share how food plays such a big part in our home life.

Welcome to our little bit of heaven by the sea. The door is open - come on in...

Jane & Myles

OUR
HOUSE

The little cottage on the hill had our names all over it. Thick stone walls, beautiful mountain views and it was even the same colour as Shells!

It didn't matter to us that it was damp and leaky, or that the rooms were poky and really dated, as we had the vision that we could make something of it.

We love to collect and to marry the old and new, so a 100-year-old cottage was the perfect project for us. It was a really exciting journey, which saw us adding a modern extension and cedar cladding, exposing the stone that was used over a century ago, pouring thick concrete floors and counters, and mixing salvage yard finds with modern art. Our goal was to treasure the old, add our personality to it, reuse as many materials as possible and create a home to be lived in, enjoyed and shared.

THE VISION

Our architect, John Wiggins, is a local surfer, really cool and really earthy. We brought him to the site and invited him to dinner. We actually never bothered to look further because it was so clear he was the right fit for us and for the house. He understood everything from the wind direction and the quality of light to the local surf lifestyle – it was a great connection.

Next we found a builder who had worked in New York and really knew about concrete. Derek Shaw understood our vision, and also contributed cool ideas. We'd come back with the oddest materials and strangest requests, but the lads went along with it. They probably thought we were mad half the time, but Derek would say: "Tell me what you want and don't worry about how to make it happen – it's my job to make it happen." By the end, they were

proud of what they'd achieved, and rightfully so.

The Look
When you take on a project like this you need to know your style. We knew from the outset that we loved industrial style. We also wanted to respect the character and history of the old cottage. All our energy went into sourcing materials that would give us the industrial feel, but also

respected the mood of the house and the location. As our house is open plan, we needed one strong identity to run through it. We also wanted to create a sense of space and freedom, so we kept doors to a minimum and opened up the ceilings to their maximum height. We stuck to raw materials. We've used concrete, stone and wood for our primary floor, walls and kitchen units. And although the quality and colour of all the woods

and stones vary, it seems to work.

We created a visual moodboard for all our areas. Everywhere we went we took pictures, tore scraps from magazines and spent days searching the internet. It's a lot of effort but worth it when you find the right piece and look you want. I think it also helps you really hone in and define your style. If you don't know what you like, then no one around you, from the builder to the

architect, will know either.

Our goal was to create an industrial-style cottage. The concrete floors were always on the cards, and they form a key part of the look. Everything followed from that. Even our kitchen has a poured concrete counter and island, with reclaimed wood for the presses. It's all about texture and feel. Because of this we've kept the colour palette of the house very muted.

The Dining Table

From our earliest conversations with John, we had a firm idea about the dining setup and even our dream table. We wanted it right next to the kitchen; we wanted the table to be long and narrow; we wanted it to fit at least 10 people; we wanted it to be handcrafted and Irish made. In a sense, the house was built around it. When we found Sean Fogarty at Rocker Lane Workshop, we found our table. Before it was delivered, people told us it would be too narrow, that its wood would clash with the timber wall and that it would dominate the space. But the day it arrived, that was it – we were finally home. We breathed a sigh of relief and put the kettle on.

The wood in the table is reclaimed – in discrete places you can find strips of red, yellow and white markings, little reminders of its former life as a basketball court. So we're not afraid to dance on it! We've gathered around it to eat, drink, cook, chat, and laugh and – lately – to work on this book.

love makes a house a home

The Kitchen

The kitchen for us was really important. We
wanted it to look great as it's such a central part
of our house, but it also needed to be functional.
It's one area you don't want to get wrong. We
created a moodboard and went from there.

The first appliance we bought was the cooker.
The instructions from Myles were: it must be gas
on top and have an electric oven. We went all
out and got a six-ring stove. Since we moved in,
it's cooked a lot of meals!

Another definite for us was open shelving.
We hate stretching in around corner presses,
opening every door looking for something. So we
took scaffold planks from the site and used them
as long shelves along one part of the kitchen.
It created a sense of space without overhead
cupboards, and it also meant we could make a
feature and add colour with our vintage cups,
glasses and eclectic vase selection.

Most counters get so clogged with appliances
that there's no work surface left, so we allowed for
a large prep island that divides the kitchen from
the dining table. This is the central workstation
and allows everyone to chat and chill while
dinner is being prepared.

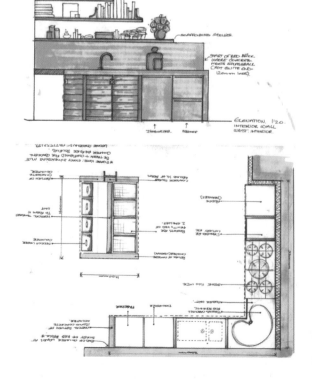

ONE MAN'S JUNK...

Although our home started its life as a cottage, we love an industrial look, which is why we used rough-hewn elements like exposed brick, concrete, stone walls and weathered timber. We layered on top of these surfaces yet more textures that call to mind an old factory...

a) The space for a bathroom door was limited, so we went to a local engineering firm who fabricated a huge sliding door. To get a suitably aged patina, we left it outside to develop a bit of rust.

b) It's super-easy to make a pendant lampshade from a length of copper wire. Just bunch it into shape around the bulb and you're all set.

c) The directional lighting in the kitchen is made up of lengths of galvanised chain, lightweight pipe and clip lamps sourced online. We sketched it for the builders and they did the rest.

d) The quirky ornaments we've attached to the garden fence were found in a derelict factory. They came from old machines, and we've just tied them on with fishing line.

e) Spray paint is the easiest way to overhaul old junk, and the kind designed for graffiti is by far the best because the range of colours is incredible. You can also get different nozzles for different effects, and it dries really, really fast. Check the wind direction before you start and put down loads of newspaper. Also be sure to wear gloves, or you'll be washing your hands for weeks. Don't forget to tag your work when you're done!

STEP OUTSIDE

Leonie Cornelius is a regular in Shells and her creativity is so apparent the minute you meet her. Leonie's a very talented garden designer running Blume House Design and we worked with her to create a wonderful grassy windblock for Shells. We were so happy we got her back to design our garden and the results are amazing. A meadow within a meadow. Here Leonie describes her grand plan for the garden.

The brief

The challenge with Myles and Jane's project was coming up with a design that could complement and do justice to this wonderful view of Knocknarea. We went for a very natural look, with an eclectic mix of old and new.

The materials

The concrete floor of the kitchen continues straight into the patio, so it's a continuous flow from inside to out and back again. The garden fence is old, rusty concrete reinforcement mesh. It just disappears because it looks so natural as it weathers. For the paths we sourced pebbles from the northwest of Ireland. Because this is their natural home, they look like they just belong. They're also very soft and informal compared to other options like gravel.

The plantings

We've used three perennial grasses because these make a garden look natural and loose rather than contrived, and they require little maintenance. The soft scheme almost resembles a meadow, and this felt like the best way to work with the dramatic wild backdrop of the mountain. *Stipa tenuissima* – often called ponytail grass – adds texture and movement. *Stipa gigantea* is a small, bushy evergreen grass. It only grows to about 40cm tall, but then the flowerheads come up to 1.5m, so they kind of float above everything else. *Anemanthele lessoniana* is another evergreen grass that goes golden in autumn, and the seed heads are gorgeous on them.

UNDER COVER

A lot of our thinking about organising our outdoor space stemmed from Myles' upbringing in Cape Town. When you grow up in a hot country, your life is outdoors. We really wanted to embrace that – despite the fact we're on the west coast of Ireland.

We're a stone's throw from the beach, so realistically you come in from the surf soaking wet and scattering sand everywhere. We realised there's no point in denying the fact that there's always going to be a stack of surfboards and wetsuits around, so wanted to fit them into our life properly with a cool shed.

We worked with a really good local carpenter who used the cedar off-cuts from the house renovation. It's super hardwearing wood so it can take the battering. He adjusted the height to accommodate our longest board, and installed a clothes rail for the neoprene. Thick wooden dowels set at an angle hold boots, gloves and hoods, while dowels with pipe cladding keep boards upright. We've got rubber mats on the floor to protect board noses and tails too. Shelving contains wax, handplanes and other equipment. In a separate compartment you'll find our bikes and everything for the barbecue. We love it – but we're not done yet. Our next project is to install an extractor fan to facilitate wetsuit drying.

POWER TO
THE SHOWER

We don't live in the warmest climate, but we do have this incredible view of Knocknarea. It seems a shame to waste it even for a minute, and that's part of the reason we installed an outdoor hot water shower. It's quite common to want to bring the outdoors in, but in this project we ended up bringing the inside out!

During the planning process, the hot shower seemed like a bit of a luxury and not that practical, but in fact it's become one of the favourite features of the house. When anyone comes to visit we eventually force people in whether they like it or not. They end up loving it, because showering outside transforms a pretty mundane daily task into a treat.

We were careful to position it in such a way that it's not overlooked – otherwise it could be a bit hard to relax. Trailing vines help create a screen, and also lend a feeling of total immersion in nature. The floor is made up of readymade decking tiles over the same concrete as the rest of our patio, with grooves directing water to the drain.

Anything exposed to the elements has to be hardwearing so we didn't even bother with a showerhead – our builders just fashioned the entire shower from one piece of lovely copper pipe. Junk shop finds fit perfectly here, like an old swimming pool ladder that we've turned into a towel rack or a bit of chipped crockery to hold the soap. For outdoor living, it's good to use things that are already a bit wrecked, because you don't end up feeling too precious about them.

"I thought: 'There is a waterfall
Upon Ben Bulben side
That all my childhood counted dear;
Were I to travel far and wide
I could not find a thing so dear.'"
– From 'Towards Break of Day' by WB Yeats

FIRE PIT PATROL

In putting together our garden, we knew we wanted a permanent fire pit because we're committed to being outdoors no matter what. We had to dismantle a 100 year-old stone shed in the house renovation, so it was great to give the old stones a new purpose by using them in the construction of the fire pit. We looked at the prevailing winds too, and were able to keep some of the shed's stone walls in place to form a natural windbreak.

For cooking on the fire pit, it's just a matter of sticking on the fuel and a grid, and off you go. But even if we're having people for dinner indoors, one of the first things we do is get the fire pit going. Gathering around and gazing into a fire is relaxing and communal – it really breaks down barriers.

After dinner, we distribute blankets and bring out candles in tins to set the scene. Now's the time for hot drinks and whiskies, and we always have a bag of marshmallows at the ready. It's consistently interesting to see that for young and old alike, the pleasure factor in roasting marshmallows is exactly the same.

MYLES' FAST BBQ FACTS

- Natural lumpwood charcoal is expensive, but because it's very hard it burns slower, holds the heat and produces much better flavour than briquettes.
- If you're cooking over wood rather than charcoal, hardwoods like ash or chestnut burn well, while softer woods like pine are less suitable.
- When you're setting up kindling remember it needs cavities of air, so arrange it either in the form of a teepee or layer it in hashtag shapes.
- Fires often suffer from limited oxygen feed, so use a bike pump as bellows beneath your barbecue to stoke it back to life.

SPRING

YOGA
BREKKIE

As friends started having babies we realised we needed to think beyond late-night dinners and come up with other informal party ideas. A yoga breakfast makes an interesting alternative, and it's perfect if you're not that confident in the kitchen as all the prep can be done in advance.

The first step is to arrange for a local yoga teacher to do a weekend morning class for you and your friends. It can benefit the teacher too because there's a chance to gain exposure to a group of potential clients. If you don't have enough space at your place, plan to use an open area – we go to the beach but a park would work just as well.

The host only needs to pick seasonal flowers to decorate the house, mix up Bircher muesli, make fresh juice, cut fabulous fruit and source some terrific breads. Everything just goes on the table – served buffet style – alongside eclectic crockery, graphic napkins and vintage spoons for the drinks and jams.

After nurturing the soul with yoga, the menu is all about nurturing the body. Then, anyone with kids or commitments will head off, while others often end up on blankets in the garden drinking herbal tea.

YOGI BREKKIE

Spring is all about a desire for healthy eating, enjoying the season and getting fit. This breakfast section is a great way to start your day with some natural foods packed with goodness, colour and slow-release energy.

BIRCHER MUESLI BREAKFAST

Packed full of goodness, Bircher muesli was developed by the Swiss. What I love about it is that you can make it up the night before and then in the morning tuck straight in. Unlike porridge, which involves pots, watching and getting it right, you can have this ready and waiting to go. So no excuses to skip brekkie!

There are many ways to make this depending on your own personal preferences for oats and fruit. We love this one, but feel free to tweak to get the balance right just for you.

SERVES 2

- 2 cups porridge/rolled oats
- 1 cup apple juice/orange juice
- 1 cup milk/yoghurt
- 1 tablespoon sugar
- Handful almonds/toasted hazelnuts
- Handful dried apricots or raisins, finely chopped
- Pinch nutmeg
- Pinch cinnamon

TO SERVE:

- 1 apple
- Honey, to taste
- Sliced fresh fruit

1 Ideally start the night before. Combine all the ingredients together in a bowl (except the honey and apple) and allow to rest in the fridge overnight or for at least one hour.

2 When ready to serve, grate one whole apple into the mix, add some honey to sweeten and give a good stir. Have a taste to see if you need a dash more juice or perhaps more yoghurt.

3 Serve with fresh fruit, yoghurt and the morning sun on your face.

JULIEN'S GLUTEN-FREE RASPBERRY AND COCONUT MUFFINS

These muffins sell really well in the Shells Little Shop. They look fantastic when you slice them open, as well as tasting amazing. This recipe will give you 12 muffins but can easily be doubled if you're having a party.

- 200g (1¾ cups) gluten-free flour, like Tritamyl
- 200g (1¾ cups) ground almonds
- 200g (2 cups) desiccated coconut
- 375g (1½ cups) caster sugar
- 375g (1½ cups) full fat yoghurt
- 3 or 4 eggs (3 large or 4 medium)
- 1 pinch baking soda
- 375g (1 cup) frozen raspberries
- 12 muffin cases

1 Preheat oven to 170C/340F.

2 Begin by mixing the sugar, yoghurt and eggs together.

3 Fold in the flour, almonds, soda and coconut.

4 Mix to form a batter and then scatter in the frozen berries. Lightly fold them through the mix.

5 Fill each muffin case up to two-thirds, allowing room to rise.

6 Bake for 35 to 40 minutes at 170C/340F – no higher or else the top of the muffin will burn.

7 Allow to cool, sprinkle with a little icing sugar on top to serve. Enjoy!

MYLES' ALTERNATIVE FRUIT PLATTERS

On my travels I've had lots of nice breakfasts. I'm always surprised when I get a little bit of fruit seasoned with some spice – it brings out the flavour. These are some of my favourites (inspired by a recent trip to Portugal).

Marinated strawberries with balsamic vinegar and mint

Sliced oranges with sugar and cinnamon

Sliced mango with brown sugar and chilli powder

Roasted grapefruit with muscovado sugar

Thinly sliced pineapple with sweet ginger syrup, lime zest and chilli

Raspberries with cracked black pepper

CHICKEN RUN

Gary Smith lives right over the road from us and keeps chickens, so we got him to tell us his tips for keeping hens and having a constant supply of delicious eggs at home.

"We started keeping chickens when a girl down the road from us got a new coop and gave us her old one. We've got a huge garden that sits there doing nothing, so we thought we'd put it to use. We've got dogs but they don't give us a lot. Well, they do – but you can't make an omelette out of love!

"We built a chicken run, but mostly we let them range about, shuffling around the hedges and pecking for bugs. We have a huge feeder where the pellets come out automatically, and every day without fail they get leftover porridge. They are mad for it! As a treat I give them handfuls of seeds mixed with corn. Then every other day, you just put a glove on and scoop the straw and sawdust out of the coop. Any mess just gets picked up that way.

"Generally when they're in full health and the right age, you'll get an egg out of every chicken – not bad! If I'm cooking something where you won't taste the egg in it, I really don't want to use one of these because they're just too good. The yolks are bright vivid yellow – gorgeous. I love poached eggs for breakfast, and there's no comparison between a supermarket egg and one of these."

Unlike a veggie patch or flower garden, hens can't be left for a week while you head off on holiday; every day they need to be fed, watered, let out in the morning and closed in at night. But the investment of your time and energy is well worth it, because eggs laid in your very own yard are like nothing you've ever tasted.

- A hen will live for 5 to 7 years on average.
- Hens begin laying eggs at 3 to 6 months.
- Typically, hens lay until they're around 3 years old.
- You need to keep at least 2 because hens are flock birds.
- Healthy hens lay around 250 eggs annually.
- Kept cool, dark and dry, eggs keep for up to 6 weeks.
- A coop for a two hens should be at least 250cm long and 150cm wide.
- Expect each hen to eat 125 to 180g of pellets, oats, wheat or maize per day.
- Hens are omnivores, so they love to snack on kitchen scraps, weeds, seeds and worms too.

OH SO SLOW SCRAMBLED EGGS
WITH FOREST MUSHROOMS AND TARRAGON

Do yourself a favour and try these scrambled eggs – makes the most awesome brekkie and is well worth the effort.

SERVES 2

- 5 or 6 eggs
- 50ml (¼ cup) cream
- Salt and pepper
- 3 tablespoons butter
- 1 tablespoon good vinegar, like aged balsamic or sherry vinegar
- 2 handfuls mushrooms (go for a variety you have not had before; often you can purchase a forest mix, which are delish)
- 2 cloves garlic, diced
- 2 tablespoons tarragon, chopped
- Dash olive oil
- To make this you will need a small pot of simmering water, a Pyrex-style glass bowl and a cake spatula.

1 Crack the eggs into the bowl, add the cream and a teaspoon of butter.
2 Gently whisk together (do not over whisk).
3 Place the bowl on top of the simmering pot of water; every now and then very gently stir with folding actions to create a scrambled egg mix.
4 Slowly, slowly, gently, gently with the eggs as they delicately scramble over the low heat. The butter will melt though, so add a little more butter for indulgence. Get those eggs really silky. Taste and season with salt and pepper.
5 This method can take up to 15 or 20 minutes of gentle folding, so meanwhile sauté the lovely mushrooms in a pan or wok with the garlic, olive oil and a knob of butter. Cook gently and again taste to season. At the end sprinkle with the fresh tarragon.
6 Butter up some thick crunchy toast, spoon on the silky eggs and sprinkle a few drops of high quality vinegar over the eggs. This helps 'cut' the buttery richness of the eggs and gives another dimension to the dish. Top with mushrooms and fresh herbs.
7 Sit down with the Sunday paper, a cup of coffee and smile as the world goes by.

BAKED EGGS EN CROUTE

So you've had fried eggs, scrambled eggs or poached. But have you had baked eggs? This is often the forgotten method. They look super fancy and there are so many different variations and combinations that you won't get bored for a while. It's also a perfect weekend dish when you have guests.

I like mine with mushrooms at the bottom and gruyere cheese on top, eaten with toast of course.

You will need ramekins for this dish, so make sure you have them, or if you are browsing in charity shops look out for the traditional egg coddlers – that's the real deal.

EQUIPMENT YOU NEED FOR THIS DISH
• Small oven-proof ramekins which can hold two eggs
• Deep roasting tin or square cake tin
• Hot kettle with boiled water
• Oven at 180C/350F

INGREDIENTS
• Butter
• Eggs (two per person)
• Salt and pepper
• Milk or cream – cream is better
• Optional extras: hard cheese, smoked salmon, spinach, mushrooms, chorizo, onions, herbs, tomato sauce, mustard and ham – or any other things you like with eggs.

1 Preheat the oven and fold a damp kitchen towel on the bottom of the roasting dish.
2 Rub the insides of the ramekins with a good layer of butter (or oil if you prefer) and add the chosen extras to the bottom.
3 Crack in the eggs (one or two) and top with a splash of milk or cream (not too much) and perhaps some extras like cheese or tomato.
4 Crack some black pepper and sprinkle some salt on top.
5 Next gently place the egg ramekins into the roasting dish; fill the roasting dish halfway up with hot water. This helps ensure even cooking of the eggs.
6 Bake for around 10 to 15 minutes, until the whites are set.
7 Remove carefully and gobble up straight away with toast or savoury muffins.

ZEST
FOR LIFE

Spring is one of my favourite seasons. Everything starts coming to life as the sun shines earlier and stays with us for longer. The usual excuses for not exercising, like 'it's too dark or too cold', go out the window.

One of the things I love doing this time of year is dusting down my vintage bike and getting out on the road. We've both got bikes which we rescued and restored from the tip. Equipment that's different and quirky will at the very least make you smile – and might make pedalling up that next killer hill a bit more fun!

I love early morning runs along the beach, before the world starts to wake up. Sometimes there are no other footprints and you feel as if you're the only person around. This year I'm training for the Coney Island Run, which is a beautiful run across the wet sand to Coney Island, so running on the beach is perfect training for me.

SUPER HEALTHY SPRING SALAD

This salad is not only bursting with flavour, but packed full of spring greens and lots of crunch.

SERVES 2
- 3 handfuls asparagus
- 1 head broccoli
- 3 handfuls mangetout
- Olive oil
- Sea salt
- 1 small fennel bulb
- 1 small onion, thinly sliced
- 1 green pepper
- Half a cucumber, deseeded and peeled

TO GARNISH
- Handful of mint
- Sprinkle of poppy seeds
- Pinch of bean sprouts

1 Bring a pot of water to the boil. Once at a rolling boil add in the asparagus, broccoli and mange tout; allow to boil for 2 minutes, then remove and rinse with cold water.
2 Drizzle the asparagus, broccoli and mange tout with olive oil and sea salt flakes.
3 Cut the fennel bulb into very thin half moons.
4 Slice the top off the pepper and pull out the seeds. Then slice the pepper into circles.
5 Using a potato pealer, peel the skin from the cucumber. Slice into thick circles and cut them in half again.
6 Mix all the ingredients together in a large bowl. Sprinkle with fresh mint, poppy seeds and bean sprouts, then drizzle with a mint and basil dressing.

MINT AND BASIL DRESSING
- 200ml (1 cup) olive oil
- 65ml (¼ cup) cider vinegar
- Salt and pepper
- Fresh mint and basil to taste

7 Combine all the ingredients in a large bowl, whisk lightly to mix and serve immediately.

SPROUT ABOUT IT

These beany bundles add nutrition and crunch to meals, and watching them grow is pretty fun too. Reaping the benefits takes only minimal effort and a handful of items found around the house.

Gather these things:

- A big jar with a wide mouth
- A piece of netting
- A rubber band
- 4 tbsp of mung beans or lentils, or a mix of both
- A bowl
- A tea towel

And then get to work:

- Put the beans in the jar
- Add 250ml cold water
- Screw on the top and leave overnight
- Drain off the water
- Position the netting over the mouth of the jar
- Fasten the netting in place with the rubber band
- Rest the jar upside down at a 45-degree angle in the bowl so extra water can drain
- Cover with a tea towel to keep the whole operation in darkness
- After a day, rinse the beans
- Repeat steps 4, 5, 6, 7 and 8 a couple of times every day
- After five days, you should have a harvest that can be added to recipes or stored in a container in the fridge

N E W
L E A S E
O F
L I F E

Upcycling is about having the creative vision to repurpose objects you love the look of into things you can use. In our house we love to give redundant pieces and materials a new lease of life.

By adapting vintage tableware you can use succulents to create an instant garden inside your home. These richly coloured plants are quite sculptural on their own, but when you pot them into random vessels you practically get a miniature art installation. They make fun place card holders or centrepieces for a dinner, and cool housewarming or hostess gifts too. Here's how you do it:

› Succulents have very shallow roots, so you don't need to do any digging – just force them into the soil with your fingers.

› These little guys hate getting waterlogged, so the best soil to use will have a bit of sandy grit mixed in to facilitate drainage – John Innes compost is a good choice.

› When larger succulents produce side shoots, just break these off and stick them in soil. They'll take root and grow like mad.

› If in doubt, don't water. Succulents don't like too much moisture, which can make them quite foolproof for anyone who struggles with more traditional houseplants. Just keep them in a sunny window!

SALT 'N' PEPPER SQUID

A lot of people only get their calamari fix in a restaurant. But it's sooooo easy to do, so why not try it at home? See our tips on page 96 on how to prepare it fresh.

SERVES 4

- 3 large or 4 medium size calamari tubes, sliced into thin rings
- 300g (2 cups) all-purpose flour
- ½ teaspoon cayenne pepper
- ½ teaspoon turmeric
- 1 teaspoon salt
- 1 teaspoon cracked black pepper
- 1 litre vegetable oil for deep frying
- Lemons to serve

1 Add all the DRY ingredients together; you now have a nice seasoned flour. Toss the calamari into the flour, making sure every bit is coated.
2 Heat the oil in a pan to just about smoking hot, around 170C/340F.
3 Drop in the squid in small batches, cooking each batch for one minute or so. Remove and place onto kitchen paper to soak up the excess oil.
4 Squeeze fresh lemon juice over the squid and gobble up quickly with some lemon mayo.

CEVICHE

Ceviche is a cold fish salad from South America. The raw ingredients get pickled in the citrus juices. It's an amazing appetizer, super healthy and packed full of flavour. Don't turn your nose up at the thought of raw fish until you've tried ceviche.

SERVES 4

- 100g/3.5oz firm white fish fillet like snapper, plaice, sea bass or hake
- 100g/3.5oz tuna fillet (ask for sustainable line-caught tuna)
- Juice of 2 limes and zest of 1 lime
- Juice of 2 lemons
- 1 tablespoon olive oil (for oilier fish use nut oil like hazelnut or sesame oil)
- 1 yellow pepper, finely diced
- 1 red chilli, sliced
- 1 small bunch coriander, roughly chopped
- 1 small bunch flat leaf parsley, roughly chopped
- 1 tomato, diced
- Salt and pepper
- A dash or two of Tabasco sauce

1 Rinse your fish under cold running water and pat dry with a kitchen towel.
2 Dice the fish into small chunks and combine all the ingredients in a large bowl. Allow this to marinate for up to an hour in the fridge, stirring halfway through.
3 Serve up in fancy glasses garnished with lime wedges and coriander. You can pimp this up with guacamole and tortilla chips.
4 Goes down really well with sunsets and Corona!

SALMON PÂTÉ

Ok, so you have some leftover cooked salmon. Only two pieces but four people coming for lunch… Hmm! Cold salmon pâté is easy-peasy and makes the perfect lunch.

SERVES 2 TO 4

- 2 cooked salmon pieces
- 2 tablespoons cream cheese
- 2 tablespoons chopped green herbs, like dill, chive or parsley
- Zest and juice of a lemon
- Salt and pepper to taste
- Pinch cayenne pepper
- 50ml (⅛ cup) extra virgin olive oil
- Thin crispy toast to serve

1 Whizz all the ingredients together in a food processor except the olive oil. Slowly drip that in while blitzing the ingredients.
2 Spoon it into ramekins and smooth over the top with a knife. For effect sprinkle some green herbs on top.
3 Let these rest in the fridge for about 20 to 30 minutes or until firm.
4 Serve with a nice side salad (make sure there's lots of cucumber in it) and some crispy hot buttered toast.

CALARAMI AND CHORIZO SALAD

A great combination.

SERVES 2

- 1 squid, sliced thinly
- 200g (7oz) fresh chorizo, diced
- 300g (approx 12) parboiled new/baby potatoes
- 100g (3 cups) washed rocket leaves (arugula)
- 50ml (⅛ cup) olive oil
- 1 lemon
- Salt and pepper

FOR THE PESTO:

- 2 bunches basil, trimmed with stalks removed
- 50g (½ cup) pine nuts
- 50g (½ cup) grated parmesan
- 150ml (⅔ cup) extra virgin olive oil
- Salt to taste

1 Bang all the pesto ingredients into a food processor and blend well. Taste and add some more salt, cheese or pepper to taste.

2 Get the pan on, nice and hot. Add a glug of olive oil and a squeeze of lemon. Toss and fry the potatoes until golden and crisp. Add a pinch of salt and pepper halfway through. Take out and allow to rest in a bowl.

3 Keeping the pan hot, toss in the chorizo and fry for a minute, then add in the squid and fry for another two minutes, tossing in the pan. Return the potatoes into the pan and stir everything together. Next add a dollop of the basil pesto and stir. Dish up into your favourite bowl and throw some fresh rocket on top. If you fancy it, add some freshly grated parmesan and some lemon zest.

4 If you've been growing edible flowers, add some for decoration and colour.

SPRING LAMB SALAD WITH HARISSA

Harissa is a spicy Tunisian chilli sauce that packs a bit of punch so use it sparingly if you're a bit sensitive to spice.

SERVES 4

400g (14oz) lamb rump (lamb steaks)

SPICY MARINADE:

- 1 teaspoon harissa paste
- 1 large garlic clove, diced
- 100ml (¼ cup) olive oil

- 1 tablespoon red wine vinegar

SALAD:

- 2 tins chickpeas
- 1 large bunch fresh mint
- 2 handfuls baby spinach
- 1 lemon, zested and juiced
- 1 red chilli, chopped
- 1 red onion, thinly sliced
- Mint, thinly sliced

DRESSING:

- 100ml (¼ cup) olive oil
- 2 teaspoons sugar
- Juice of one lemon
- Salt and pepper
- Mint, thinly sliced

1 Begin by making a nice paste with the harissa, garlic, oil and vinegar. Gently massage the paste into the lamb steaks (lamb chops can also be used) and allow them marinate gently for over an hour.

2 Grill or pan-fry the lamb to your preferred liking. I like mine medium rare, brushing the meat with more marinade halfway through. Allow the meat to rest for a few minutes before serving.

3 For the salad, grab a bowl and toss in the drained chickpeas, spinach leaves, chilli, mint and onion. Season with salt and pepper, swirling it all around. Only add the dressing at the very last minute as the lemon juice will 'cook' the spinach.

4 The dressing is very simple: combine the lemon juice, olive oil, sugar, mint, salt and pepper into an old jam jar and shake hard. Pour over the plated-up lamb salad. Top with fresh mint. Best served with cucumber yoghurt, warm pitta breads and a light Pinot Grigio.

EASY PEASY GNOCCHI

What are you going to do with that leftover
mashed potato? Turn it into gnocchi of course!

SERVES 4
- 4 medium potatoes, boiled or baked then mashed
- 1 to 1.5 cups (130–195g) strong flour
- 1 tablespoon olive oil
- Salt and pepper

1 Grab a large bowl and begin by mixing your flour slowly into your potato together
  with the seasoning and olive oil to create a dough-like consistency. The amount of
  flour varies, depending on the water content of your mashed potato. You can also
  add herbs or spices like oregano or sage to the flour for a fancier meal. The best way
  to mix is by using your hands; you want to get a consistency where you can roll the
  dough into small balls. To avoid gummy, rubbery gnocchi, do not overwork the dough.
2 Test by dropping a small ball of dough into boiling water; if it rises to the top that's
  good, but if it falls apart and crumbles just add more flour.
3 Turn the dough onto a floured surface and roll out pieces of the dough into long rope-
  like strands, just thicker than a pencil. Remember, gnocchi will expand a little when
  cooked.
4 To create your gnocchi, slice the rope strands into individual segments about two
  inches long (20mm). For traditional effect, roll each piece with a fork to create
  distinctive ridges. This helps the sauce cling on for more flavour.
5 Toss batches into rapidly boiling water for a minute or two until the gnocchi rise to the
  top. Scoop out with a slotted spoon and let them rest on some baking parchment.
  They can be used straight away with any recipe, or pop them in the freezer for later.
6 I find the best way to serve gnocchi is to boil them, let them cool and then pan fry
  them with butter!

SPRING GREENS AND GNOCCHI

When spring is in the air, eat a bowl full of vegetarian goodness packed with healthy green vegetables.

SERVES 4

- 100g/3.5oz butter
- 500g/1lb ready-made gnocchi
- 2 cloves garlic, diced
- 1 small bunch fresh sage, roughly chopped
- Juice of 2 lemons and zest of 1
- Spring greens mix: asparagus tips, peas, fava beans, green beans, sugar snaps, runner beans, baby broccoli shoots
- Handful of rocket leaves
- Parmesan shavings
- Salt and pepper

1 Begin by cooking or steaming all your spring vegetables until 'al dente'. Plunge them into ice water to help maintain their vibrant green colour and also to keep them from overcooking in their own heat.

2 Next grab a large frying pan and begin to melt the butter. As it starts to foam, add the garlic and chopped sage. Baste the sage leaves with hot butter to get them nice and crispy. Next throw in the gnocchi, but watch the heat – perhaps turn it down a little to prevent the butter from burning. You want the butter to be a nutty brown colour. Add the lemon juice and zest, followed by the vegetables. Stir all around so everything gets the flavour of the buttery sage. Season with lots of salt and cracked black pepper, then serve up into bowls garnished with rocket leaves and lashings of parmesan cheese.

3 Goes down really well with light, crisp Pinot Grigio, followed by figs and a cheese board. Cheers!

SAY CHEESE

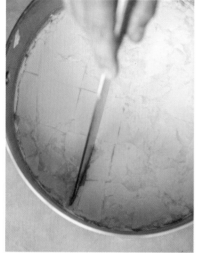

Cheese making is a great hobby to get into, especially if you're into cooking and want to use your kitchen in different ways. You can make a soft cheese with hardly any equipment. Try this simple project as an experiment; if you find you like making cheese, then you can invest in various bacterial cultures to make rind washes and hard and semi-soft cheeses.

1 Begin with two litres (1.7 quarts) of milk – milk from goats, sheep or cows will work.
2 Heat this up to just below a simmer.
3 Now cool it to lukewarm and add two or three drops of rennet, which you can buy at a health food store.
4 After an hour things will start to go wobbly. At this point, cut the curds into big blocks by striking a hashtag shape with a clean knife.
5 Pour the contents of the pot into the centre of a muslin cloth. Add salt, pepper and thyme if you like, then tie this into a ball.
6 Hang the cloth parcel so that the liquid can drip off into a sink. The curds and whey can now separate.
7 Hang it for a day or two.
8 You've now got a simple soft cheese to spread on crackers or sandwiches and serve with wine.
9 If you leave the cheese a few more days in a dark, cool place, it will go crumbly – perfect for a salad.

TRY THIS – ADD YOUR HOMEMADE CHEESE TO:

- Hot buttered sourdough toast and fruit chutney
- Omelettes and fritatta – for that extra flavour and richness
- Mix it into potato gratin
- And make sure when people are eating it that you tell them you made it too!

BORN
SLIPPY

There's more to life than thrusters and logs – a truly good surfer aims to be
an all-round waterman. Alternative surfcraft not only offer another way
to slide into the ocean, but their cool materials and shapes make them
gorgeously aesthetic design objects in their own right. We like to mix
things up and try out different surfcraft from time to time. Here's a peek at
the alternatives that we keep to hand.

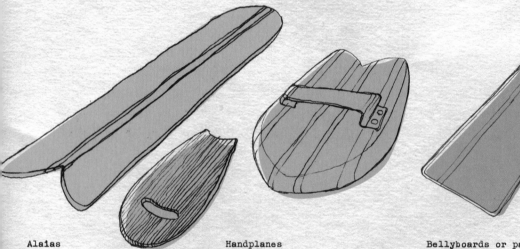

Alaias

The ancient Hawaiians rode
wooden surfboards called alaias.
These finless water vehicles
require quite a bit of skill
to ride. Because an alaia is
incredibly thin, it barely
planes the water. In contrast
to a modern surfboard, the
sensation is slipping on top of
the surface rather than being
stuck into the wave. Finless
surfing consequently opens you
up to different manoeuvres like
360s and wraparound sprays.
The absence of fins also means
there's minimal drag, so it
gives you a very, very fast
ride.

Handplanes

In mainstream surfing, you only
really get one perspective of
wave dynamics – from the top.
Bodysurfing on the other hand
broadens your understanding
of how water works. In its
purest form it doesn't need
any equipment at all – just a
body and some surf. But wearing
swim fins will help propel
you into the wave and using a
handplane will give you a much
longer ride. That's because its
buoyancy elevates your body
just enough to keep you in the
crest of the wave. Besides being
one of the cheapest and most
portable watercraft you can get,
it's tons of fun.

Bellyboards or paipos

Archival photographs of the
Nobel-winning Irish playwright
George Bernard Shaw show him
bellyboarding at Muizenberg
in South Africa. This is the
easiest and least technical form
of surfing that exists – if you
can stand in a shallow beach
break then you can do it. The
idea is to wait for a foamy wave
to break, then launch yourself
onto the board and ride straight
towards the shore. Thanks to its
hard, flat surface and finless
construction, this bentwood
watercraft – known as a paipo
in Hawaii – provides a fast,
planing slide.

..Oh I do like to live beside the seaside

SARAH'S SPECIAL OCCASION TREATS

Sarah Elvey runs the ship in Shells Café. When we discovered her secret baking skills we just couldn't resist asking her to share her recipes. Sarah can create magic in her home kitchen, and her lovely Polka Dot cake and macarons are perfect for any occasion, especially Mother's Day, Easter and birthdays.

POLKA DOT CAKE

- 2 cups (450g) sugar
- 1lb (450g) butter
- 3 cups (450g) self-raising flour
- 8 eggs, lightly beaten
- Food colouring
- 2 teaspoons vanilla extract
- 3 tablespoons milk

1 Preheat the oven to 160C/320F and have three greased and lined 18cm (7-inch) round tins ready.

2 Cream the butter and sugar together until light and fluffy.

3 Add half of the egg and vanilla extract and half of the flour to the creamed butter and sugar.

4 Mix slowly until incorporated then add the other half and the milk.

5 Divide the batter in two and split one half into two bowls – or as many bowls as needed for different coloured dots. Add food colouring to each of the smaller bowls of batter.

6 Place coloured batters in a cake pop mould and bake until golden and cooked through; knock out and leave to cool on a wire rack.

7 Meanwhile spread some of the white cake batter into each of the tins and dot the coloured balls around the tin. Top with rest of batter ensuring that the coloured balls are covered.

8 Bake for 20 minutes or until fully cooked. Test with a skewer but be sure to put the skewer into the light cake and not one of the already cooked balls. Place on a wire rack to cool.

9 Sandwich together with a fabulous buttercream and cover completely. The wow factor comes when you slice into it.

MACARONS

Sarah's macarons are a delight, give this recipe a try and you won't be disappointed.

MAKES 20 MACARONS

- 170g (1⅓ cups) icing (powdered) sugar
- 160g (1¼ cups) ground almonds
- 120ml (approx ½ cup) egg whites from 4 medium eggs, divided into 2 equal batches
- 160g (¾ cup) granulated sugar
- 1 teaspoon red food colouring
- 75g (¼ cup) strawberry jam
- You will also need a sugar thermometer and a piping bag

1 Preheat the oven to 170C/340F and line two baking trays with baking parchment. Put the icing sugar and ground almonds into the bowl of a food processor and pulse until fully combined. Sift this mixture into a large bowl, discarding any small particles that stay in the sieve.

2 Add the first batch of egg whites to the almond mixture, mix together to form a paste, then set aside.

3 Put 50ml (¼ cup) water and the granulated sugar in a small pan set over a medium heat. Bring to the boil and have a sugar thermometer ready. Meanwhile, put the second batch of egg whites into a clean grease-free bowl (this is best done using a freestanding electric mixer) and whisk on medium.

4 When the syrup in the pan approaches about 118C/245F on the sugar thermometer, start whisking the whites on high speed. Once the syrup registers 118C/245F, pour the syrup slowly down the side of the bowl of egg whites, avoiding the beaters.

5 Continue to whisk the meringue on high until the mixture has cooled slightly and the bowl is no longer hot to the touch but is still warm. Add the food colouring and whisk to combine.

6 Scrape the meringue onto the almond mixture and gently fold together. It is important not to over mix at this stage. The batter should fall in a thick ribbon from the spatula, fading back into the batter within 30 seconds. If it doesn't, fold a few more times.

7 Add the batter to a piping bag with a 1cm (½ inch) plain piping nozzle. Pipe rounds about 2.5cm (1 inch) in diameter onto prepared baking trays. Leave to rest for 30 minutes or until the macarons have developed a skin and are no longer sticky, then bake for 12 minutes. Immediately slide the parchment onto the work surface and allow the macarons to cool for a few minutes before gently peeling them off the paper.

8 Fill the centre with jam and sandwich together. Chill overnight before serving, allowing macarons to come to room temperature before enjoying.

ROSES – TO GO!

To get a garden going when you move into a new house requires petal power. Garden designer Leonie Cornelius helped us out with this great housewarming how-to that you can do any time of year.

(1) Invite friends for a party to celebrate your garden-to-be, and ask them to bring a cutting from their favourite rose bush.

(2) Guests without roses of their own could bring wild cuttings instead. Roses flourishing by a local roadside are likely to not only be hardy, but will also be better suited to your environment than a plant from the garden centre that's been raised in a polytunnel abroad.

(3) Clippings should be about 15cm (6 inches) and contain two growth buds. Ask each friend to put his or her clipping into an opaque vase or cup about two weeks before the party to give it time to form a root.

(4) On the day of the party, cuttings can be stuck straight into the ground. As long as you keep the soil moist, you have every reason to expect a real rose garden to appear the following year.

FRINGE TASSEL GARLAND

Give your party an extra wow factor with this gorgeous garland, here are Shelly's tips on how to make it.

You will need:

- Tissue paper sheets (five sheets makes two tassels; 10 to 15 tassels will make a 1.5m (5 foot) garland)
- Tacky glue (optional)
- Scissors
- Ribbon trim – as much as you need for the length of garland

Instructions:

- Layer like colours of tissue paper, and fold the sheets over once.
- Lay folded sheets on cutting mat with folded edge on top, and use scissors to cut in half vertically. This will provide enough for two tassels. On each half, cut 1.5cm wide (1/2 inch) strips up to the centre fold, stopping 2.5cm (1 inch) from the centre.
- Unfold sheets of tissue paper. Starting with centre of stack, twist strips inward. Keep twisting gently until you have about 10 to 12cm (4 to 5 inches) of twisted tissue in the centre.
- Fold twisted centre over ribbon, and twist tissue ends until you have four or five tight twists.
- If you prefer, put glue on last twist of tissue paper and allow to dry completely.
- Fluff or separate each individual hanging strip to give each tassel a full look.
- Use scissors to trim tassels to desired length.
- Repeat with different colours and textures. Cut tassels to different lengths, and use a variety of rope trim to achieve a layered look.

SUMMER

THE GREAT SUMMER PARTY

We love little summer get-togethers. Mostly they're spontaneous, as you can never guarantee the weather. We want to encourage you to get outside, entertain and impress your friends, but do it with ease, where you as the host also get to enjoy the sunshine and the free living. Here are some ideas that work well for us and that we're always getting asked how to do.

- Summer fruit punch
- Snacks and dips
- Summery salads with a twist
- Barbecued vegetables
- The alternative barbecue
- Barbecue without the barbecue
- The extras: wildflowers, flowers in ice cubes, grilled marshmallows - and the claw!

BBQ VEGETABLES

It's not very often I say this, but barbecues aren't just for meat! Grilling or slow cooking veggies over hot coals gives them a beautiful, smoky flavour.

I like to use soft vegetables, like peppers, onions and aubergines, or sliced thin portions of fennel, sweet potatoes or pumpkin.

CORN ON THE COB

The most popular vegetable for the barbecue is corn on the cob. Just pop them on the grill and rotate gently every few minutes. The barbecue sweetens the kernels nicely. Serve hot with salty butter.

ASPARAGUS

Aspargus literally takes seconds to cook. As soon as the meat is cooked roll out a couple of bunches of asparagus on top of the grill. Keep an eye on them, roll them around every 20 seconds or so. They should be done in under three minutes. Pop them into a dish, sprinkle with salt and a knob of butter.

PEPPERS

Pop a couple of whole peppers on the side of the grill while you barbecue away. Turn them slowly. Peppers take a bit longer and are juicy and delicious sliced up over the salad or eaten as they are. No seasoning needed.

FOIL WRAPPED POTATOES

Grab a potato per guest. Pop the potatoes into a bowl, drizzle with olive oil and a generous sprinkle of salt. Get your hands oily and give the bowl a good stir. Make sure all the potatoes get a nice coating with the oily salt. Individually wrap each potato with foil and toss directly onto the hot coals just before you put the barbecue grid on. After 20 minutes turn the potatoes once. Leave for another 15 to 20 minutes depending on the size of the potato and the heat of the fire. Poke a skewer through one of the potatoes; if it slides through easily they are done! Keep them wrapped in a bowl until serving. It's easier if the guests do the unwrapping.

OTHER IDEAS:

- Foil-wrapped onions, peeled but left whole - cook for 20 minutes on hot coals
- Sliced sweet potato with honey in foil pockets
- Mixed vegetable kebabs on a stick - I like to use softer vegetables, like courgette, peppers, mushrooms and cherry tomatoes; brush with oil beforehand, then baste with butter halfway through cooking
- Big wedges of grilled pineapple on the barbecue goes down really well, especially with chicken and barbecue sauce

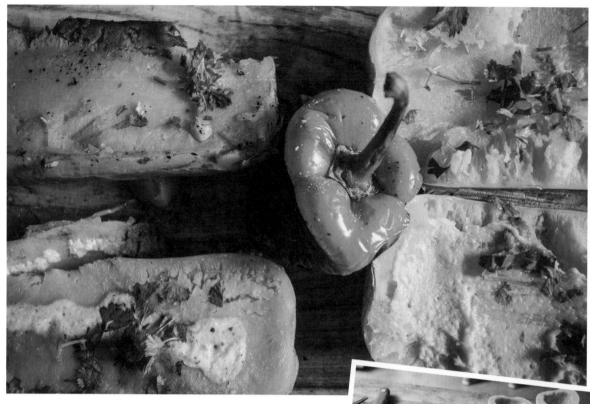

STUFFED BUTTERNUT SQUASH

Butternut squash cooked on the coals is one of my favourite things to eat. To get this right, especially if you are doing a large barbecue, I would generally make a separate fire or hot coals just to cook the squash/potatoes/onions. I like to do one sweet and one savoury option.

- 1 butternut squash should serve six to eight people. With good hot coals, cooking time is around 45 to 60 minutes turning only a few times.

1 Split the squash lengthways with a large knife and scoop out the pocket of seeds.
2 Fill the empty pockets with one of the following: feta cheese and hummus, or syrup and peanut butter.
3 Close up the squash to make it whole again. Wrap tightly with two layers of foil.
4 Place directly onto hot coals.
5 Cook until soft to the touch, around 45 minutes or so. You only need to turn it a few times during cooking.
6 To serve, unwrap and scoop out the stuffed pockets and spread over the squash. Slice and serve piping hot. Any leftovers make for a fantastic salad the next day.
7 This is a wonderful treat and should be given a go. Very rewarding, this may be the best thing at your barbecue!

FIRE PIT TOASTIES

Fire pit toasties might sound a bit strange but they are some of the best and tastiest sandwiches I've ever had. I make these every time I barbecue. They're a great finger food type starter, perfect for lads and vegetarians. Give it go, you won't regret it. One thing though, you will need a 'folding grid', also known as a box grid or swivel grid. You can easily get one online or at a good DIY or home store. Alternatively, look out for a fish grid.

SERVES 6

- 12 slices white bread, buttered on the outside
- 2 tablespoons Dijon mustard
- Cheddar cheese, sliced
- 3 tomatoes, sliced
- 1 onion, raw and thinly sliced

1 Make up the sandwiches using the buttered bread. Be sure to keep the butter on the outside. Thinly spread mustard on the inside, then layer on the sliced (not grated) cheese, tomato and onion.
2 Brush the grid with oil and 'lock' in your sandwiches.
3 Quickly barbecue over hot coals, swivelling the grid several times to get a nice toasted golden colour.
4 The barbecue 'smokes' the sandwiches and gives them a wonderful flavour.
5 Make sure you have a good space to go to with the hot sandwiches. Open up the grid, slice and serve!

Smoking fish is really cool, as it takes a normal piece of fish to a new level with a richer, deeper flavour. Smoking your own gives a great sense of satisfaction and you really appreciate that new flavour. If you have friends around it's great to get everyone involved in the process... No one minds waiting for dinner when they've learned a new skill.

There are two methods used in smoking fish: hot and cold. Cold smoking is a more involved process, but hot smoking is something you can try yourself with only a few simple materials.

HOLE-Y SMOKES

Make it
Source a rectangular metal biscuit tin. Flip the tin upside down and use a hammer and nail to perforate the bottom – you want loads of holes. Now flip it back over and fill it halfway with wood chips or shavings, which you can obtain from a local joiner. Alternatives you could use include pine needles or twigs.

Light it
A good-sized tin will fit a couple of fish; just lay your fish on top of the fuel or prop it up on two pieces of kindling if you prefer. You need a fierce heat to get things going, so a match won't do – use a blowtorch instead. Next, take a deep breath and blow hard to get the fire started. Now replace the tin's lid.

Cook it
Every so often check to make sure the fuel inside is smouldering, and relight it if needed. It's also a good idea to put the whole tin on your barbeque or a fire pit. After 15 or 20 minutes, remove the fish from your tin. (If your fillets are quite thick and haven't cooked all the way through, you can always finish off cooking them quickly in a pan.) Last, but not least, dig in and enjoy the lovely smoky flavour.

COLA PULLED PORK

Invented in America,
this is delicious!

TRY THESE IDEAS FOR SERVING:

- Pulled pork with apple Waldorf salad wraps
- Pulled pork sandwich with Applewood cheese and butterhead lettuce
- Pulled pork with refried rice and pineapple topped with fresh coriander
- Pulled pork tacos with barbecued corn on the cob
- Pulled pork with baked potato (it's great to bake potatoes with the pork), topped with crème fraîche and crispy sage

SERVES 8 TO 10

- 1 big pork shoulder on the bone (any big joint will do)
- 500ml (2 cups) barbecue sauce
- 2 onions, chopped
- 500ml (2 cups) apple juice/Coke
- 1 tablespoon mixed spice/allspice
- 3 bay leaves
- 1 stick of celery, chopped
- 1 carrot, chopped
- Salt and pepper
- 1 massive oven-proof pot or a very deep tray if using the belly cut

1 Preheat oven to 150C/300F.
2 Lightly score the skin and fat of the pork joint with a sharp knife and rub lots of salt, pepper and allspice over it. Give it a good massage.
3 In a deep tray or oven-proof pot, place the chopped carrots, celery and onion into the bottom and pop in the joint of pork. Pack it in nicely for a long bake.
4 Add the bay leaf and Coke and half the barbecue sauce.
5 Next add water so that the joint is two-thirds covered up with a nice dark spiced stock.
6 Cover tightly with a lid or foil and place in the oven for at least 6 to 8 hours.
7 Low and slow is the key here.
8 Check after 4 hours, baste the juices over the joint or turn it over if it is looking dry on top. Re-seal with foil.
9 After a very long time, take the joint out and give the meat a tug, it should pull off nice and easy. If not – back into the oven.
10 Allow to rest for about 30 minutes or so, then transfer the pork onto a tray.
11 Transfer the stock into a pot to reduce down to a nice sticky consistency.
12 With a pair of tongs and a fork, pull the meat off the bone. It should break off in long strands – basically attack the meat with a fork.
13 If it's quite fatty cut away the large bits but stir in some of the smaller bits of fat.
14 Transfer the pulled meat into a bowl and add in some more barbecue sauce or reduced stock to flavour.
15 Ready to serve!

HOME MADE
MARSHMALLOWS

What a great surprise you will get when you bite into your homemade marshmallows. There's a certain quality and texture you get by making your own that outshines any shop-bought marshmallows. We love to use rose water instead of vanilla – it's like a super-soft Turkish delight!

Bear in mind you will need a sugar thermometer.

- 455g (2½ cups) sugar
- 1 tablespoon golden syrup/honey
- 200ml (1 cup) water
- 2 large eggs, whites only
- 9 sheets gelatine (16g or ½oz), soaked in 140ml (½ cup) water
- Red food colouring
- 1 teaspoon vanilla or rose water syrup

FOR DUSTING:
- 2 tablespoons icing sugar
- 2 tablespoons cornflour

1 Begin by placing the sugar, syrup and water in a heavy-based pan and bring to the boil. Continue cooking until it reaches 127C/260F.
2 Watch out as this is VERY HOT, so no kids should come near this.
3 Meanwhile beat the egg whites until stiff peaks are formed.
4 Slowly add the gelatine into the hot sugar. Mix, but watch out as it can easily over boil. Transfer into a jug for easier pouring.
5 While still whisking the eggs, slowly drizzle the hot syrup into the bowl. The mixture will become shiny and start to thicken. Add the rose extract and continue to whisk for a further 10 minutes or so until it holds its shape well.
6 Lightly oil a shallow baking tray, dust with the icing sugar and cornflour and pour in the whipped marshmallow mixture. Flatten it out with a wet palette knife and allow to set for an hour or two at room temperature.
7 Once set, turn out and cut into blocks. Re-dust with the icing sugar and cornflour mix.
8 Keep in the fridge, as these will dissolve slowly.
9 Sit down and enjoy with your favourite DVD and sweet liqueur, or gift-up with a bunch of roses.

THE CLAW

**Roasting marshmallows over a fire isn't easy – there's a definite
art to it. It's nostalgic, fun, sweet and sticky,**

1. First off, you need to get the right marshmallows – don't get the
   multi-coloured twisty ones, go for traditional pink and white
   ones.
2. Get a long stick, sharpen it and burn the end in the fire to
   harden it further.
3. Pop one marshmallow on at a time, don't be greedy!
4. Hot coals are better for roasting over than flames. Roast well,
   rotating steadily to get an even crust. When the marshmallow
   catches on fire retrieve and blow. ALWAYS COMPARE ROASTED
   MARSHMALLOWS AMONGST OTHER ROASTERS, LOOKING FOR
   PERFECT CRUST PERFECTION.
5. Now for the 'Claw': Bring your free arm above your crispy
   marshmallow and make a crane-like claw with your hand.
   Then, as if you're a crane in a car dump, retrieve the outer crust
   of your marshmallow by gently squeezing and pulling, leaving
   a nice gooey blob behind on the stick.
6. Raise the claw towards your lips and blow hard into the open
   end of the crust – this will open it up and cool it down.
7. Place the marshmallow crust on your tongue, then crush it
   against the roof of your mouth and await sweet barbecued joy.
8. Eat the rest of the sticky, roasted marshmallow directly from
   the stick.
9. Repeat until you have had one too many!

PORK AND SAGE BURGERS WITH CELERY SALAD

So you've ticked the box with beef burgers – now try a little pork burger to tickle the taste buds. Pork is cheaper than beef and some say it's healthier on the heart too.

CELERY SALAD

- ½ cucumber, peeled, deseeded and sliced
- 1 green apple, diced
- 1 head of celery, roughly chopped
- 2 tablespoons whole almonds or walnuts, crushed

FOR THE DRESSING

- 2 tablespoons white wine vinegar
- 3 tablespoons rapeseed oil
- 1 tablespoon brown sugar
- 1 teaspoon Dijon mustard
- Salt and pepper

1 Grab an old jam jar, place all the dressing ingredients inside, and shake, shake, shake it! Voilà – dressing done.
2 Combine all the salad ingredients into your favourite bowl, add the dressing and stir everything around to marry the flavours.

MAKES FOUR BIG BURGERS OR SIX SMALLER ONES

- 700g/1.5lb pork mince
- 100g/3.5oz bacon lardons
- Small handful sage, chopped
- 2 garlic cloves, finely diced
- 2 tablespoons Dijon mustard
- 1 tablespoon Worcester sauce
- 1 egg
- Salt and pepper

GARNISH

- 4 to 6 slices smoked cheddar cheese
- 4 to 6 crispy iceberg leaves
- 2 tomatoes, sliced
- Sliced gherkins
- 3 tablespoons mayonnaise
- 1 tablespoon wholegrain mustard
- 4 soft flour baps

1 Begin by frying your lardons in a hot pan and rendering the fat out until they become crispy and brown. Next throw in the sage and fry with the bacon for a further minute.
2 Drain off excess fat and place to one side.
3 Grab a large bowl to make up your pork mix. Crack in the egg and add all ingredients, including the sage and crispy lardons; season with plenty of salt and pepper. Mix together well, getting your hands nice and meaty! Divide the mix into four or six portions. Make round balls of mince and gently pat them flat to form burger patties. If you have time, pop them into the fridge for half an hour so they firm up a little.
4 Pan fry gently for around four to five minutes on each side, turning only once. Don't be too fussy. To prevent dryness, use a spoon to baste them in their juices. Don't forget to put smoked cheese on top near the end of cooking.
5 Build each burger with mustard, mayonnaise, crispy cold lettuce, fresh tomato and gherkins. Then tuck in with celery salad, corn on the cob and cold cider!

WATERMELON, MINT AND FETA SALAD WITH A TWIST

Sounds wrong, we know, but give this a go at summer barbecues and you won't be disappointed. A total crowd pleaser and so easy to make.

If you really want hassle-free, then stick with the basics of the watermelon, mint and feta with a twist of lime. But the extra ingredients in this are worth the little bit of effort for sure. This is like eating a rainbow – so juicy, fresh and zingy.

SERVES 2

- 1 small red onion
- Juice of 3 limes
- ½ large watermelon (sweet and ripe)
- 250g (1 cup) feta cheese
- 1 bunch fresh flat leaf parsley
- 1 bunch fresh mint, chopped
- 4 tablespoons extra virgin olive oil
- 100g (½ cup) pitted black olives
- Black pepper, to season

1 Peel and halve the red onion, cut into very fine half moons and put into a small bowl to steep with the lime juice. This will take the edge off the raw onion taste.

2 Remove the rind and pips from the watermelon and cut into large bite-size chunks.

3 Cut the feta into similarly sized pieces and put them both into a large, wide, shallow bowl.

4 Tear off sprigs of parsley and add to the bowl along with the chopped mint.

5 Add the marinated onions, along with their pink juices, over the salad in the bowl. Add the oil and olives, then use your hands to toss the salad very gently so that the feta and melon don't lose their shape. Add a good grinding of black pepper and taste to see whether the dressing needs more lime.

6 Don't forget to eat the other half of the watermelon the next morning; this will refresh the senses and hydrate if you've gone a little overboard the night before.

BLACK MUSCAT GRAPE AND FRIED CHORIZO SALAD

The Forgotten Grape. All year round you can get average red and white grapes to eat and make things with. But at the end of summer there comes a beautiful small dark grape called the Muscat grape. Sweet and extra delicious, this is perfect in a spicy salad.

SERVES 2
- 1 small bag of mixed baby leaf/rocket salad (arugula)
- 100g (4oz) fresh, uncooked chorizo, sliced
- 2 tablespoons sundried tomato, chopped
- 1 large handful Muscat grapes, washed and sliced in half
- 50g (1 cup) soft goats cheese or feta
- 1 small chilli, de-seeded, diced into small bits
- 30g (approx 3) sliced pickled peppers from a jar, or sweet peppadews

DRESSING
- 3 tablespoons olive oil
- 1 tablespoon red wine vinegar
- 2 dashes Tabasco
- 1 teaspoon honey/brown sugar
- Salt and pepper to season

Pop all the ingredients into a jam jar, shake hard for about a minute

BALSAMIC REDUCTION
- 100ml (½ cup) balsamic vinegar
- 2 tablespoons sugar

1 Bring the balsamic vinegar and sugar to a hard boil for five minutes and allow to cool.
2 To make up the salad toss the jam jar dressing, peppers, sundried tomato, chilli and leaves together in a bowl.
3 Pan fry the chorizo and scatter on top of the leaves. Sprinkle lots of grapes on and then lightly place the cheese in the salad.
4 Finish the plate off by drizzling the balsamic reduction over the salad.
5 Voilà – tuck in!

PARTY TIME!

Whatever the occasion, get your party started by having your drinks ready beforehand. Here are a couple of crowd pleasers.

ONE GIANT MOJITO JUG

Everybody loves a mojito, so try this recipe for 12:

- A large container that can hold 5 litres (4.4 quarts). A stainless steel pot is always good.
- 3 massive bunches of mint (the more the better)
- 16 limes, diced
- 1 bottle (750ml) good white rum
- 2 litres (1.7 quarts) soda water
- 12 tablespoons of sugar with a splash of water
- Lots of ice

1 Begin by melting the sugar with 3 tablespoons of water and let it simmer for ten minutes to form a sugary syrup.
2 Grab your pot and add in the chopped limes, one third of the mint (leaves only, no stalks) and the sugar syrup, then bash, squash and bruise with the bottom of the rum bottle or a potato masher, to release all the mint and lime oils that give flavour to the cocktail.
3 Add the bottle of rum and soda water, a few blocks of ice (too much ice will dilute the flavours) and another third of your mint (this time keep the stalks on). Stir it all up.
4 Get your glasses ready by filling them with ice, a stalk of mint (the final third of mint) and a lime wheel to garnish.
5 Ladle in the mix to order: Top with lemonade for a sweet tooth, float a little dark rum on top for a traditional finish, or add a few dashes of Angostura bitters to enhance the flavour.
6 Enjoy the party!

SUMMER FRUIT PUNCH
(IN A BUCKET)

You can't have a summer party without a good fruit punch. And this punch packs a punch and definitely gets you a little fruity. The best bit is eating all the alcohol-soaked fruit at the bottom of the bucket.

- You will need a 10 litre (2.5 gallon) bucket, sterilised with Milton or boiling water.
- Small watermelon, skinned and diced
- 1 pineapple, peeled, cored and diced
- 4 sweet apples, peeled and diced
- 4 alternative fruits, like pears or plums, diced (just don't use banana)
- 2 oranges, diced – with skin on!
- 3 small punnets of mixed berries, like strawberries, raspberries or blueberries
- A couple of handfuls of fresh mint

LIQUIDS
- 2 bottles (750ml each) of flavoured vodka or white rum
- 1 bottle white wine, something not too dry
- 1 1.5 litre (1.3 quarts) bottle lemonade/Sprite/7UP
- 1 bottle soda water or apple juice (use apple juice if you like a sweeter cocktail)
- Ice, lots of it

1 Sterilise the bucket with boiling hot water. To make it pretty use some cool wrapping paper on the outside. Choose something bright and colourful – just like the punch!
2 Dice up the fruit, but remember to use a different chopping board to the ones you use to chop garlic!
3 Add the chopped fruit, all the liquid (keep a little back in case you like to adjust the taste), most of the berries and stir in most of the mint (hold some back for decoration).
4 Give everything a good stir and allow to sit for an hour or two for everything to mingle and marry.
5 Just before the guests arrive give it a taste and add a splash more alcohol or mixer if required. Then pile in the ice to chill the mix.
6 Fill the bucket to the top with ice, for effect.
7 Arrange your glasses next to the bucket and a "help yourself" ladle. To really make it cool, use old glass jam jars and colourful paper straws.
8 Sprinkle the remaining berries and mint on top to make it look pretty for serving.

FRESH IDEAS

We love to have freshly cut flowers in the house, as nothing shouts summer more than a colourful bouquet in a vintage vase. Annette Coleman supplies us with wildflowers at Shells, through her business Flowers from My Garden. We asked her for easy tips for harvesting and keeping cut blooms.

- When you go out into the garden to pick flowers, a basket might look pretty but a jam jar filled with water does a better job. Especially when it's sunny out, flowers will start to suffer just as soon as they're cut, so allow them to start slurping up water as soon as possible.
- Anything with a woody, heavy stem like a rose should be cut at an angle. These kinds of plants can struggle to drink enough, so this technique exposes more of the inside of the stem to water.
- When you're cutting annuals, find the longest stem and cut it right at the base; this will help strengthen the plant.
- Many stems start to close over a little bit, so cut them off again once you've got them into the house. Leave them for an hour or so before starting to make your arrangement.
- Poppies and tulips have a tendency to droop, so try this fix. Once you've picked them, seal the very tips of the stems by exposing them to boiling hot water from the kettle for six to eight seconds.
- You can give your bouquet some nutrition by adding to the water a big pinch of sugar and a drop of vinegar, a squirt of lemon juice with sugar, or even an aspirin!
- A tiny drop of bleach will help keep your jug or vase – and the water in it – nice and clean.
- Change the water every couple of days to keep your flowers feeling perky.

To attract butterflies and bees, let your garden go a bit crazy – don't be too precious about keeping things pristine and trimmed. These pollinators will appreciate it, and they'll pay you back by bringing a lively little buzz to your environment. They like bright colours and strong fragrances. If you want to make things easy for yourself, Buddleia couldn't be easier to grow and is a favourite of bees, moths and butterflies – in fact in some places it's known as the butterfly bush.

GOOD TO GROW

If you like cooking, then it would be crazy not to grow herbs in your garden. In the shop at Shells we stock dried herbs from Brian and Ellie at Trimilawn Farm. They also sell fresh herb plants at local markets, and will even grow varieties to order, which is great for chefs and foodies.

The garden containers we built at Shells hold potted plants, and it's so easy to swap these around with the changing seasons. It also lifts the eye up above the carpark and carries your gaze out to the sea. At home our raised bed is made from scaffolding off-cuts from the renovation, and we've filled this with soil and planted a little kitchen garden directly into it.

Wherever you decide to put your herbs, consider the soil type. For example in the west of Ireland, we mainly have heavy, compact soil. Mints, comfrey and lemon bergamot tend to flourish here. Plants that do well in sandy, freely draining soil include Mediterranean herbs such as rosemary, thyme, chamomile and lavender. And if you've got a mix of clay and sand – which we would call a loam soil – then herbs like chives, parsley and sage are ideal.

HERB FLAVOURS

Trimilawn Farm has hooked us up with some fantastic and unusual herb flavours – here are a few offbeat options worth sourcing for your own growing, cooking and eating efforts:

Angelica – used to flavour liqueurs and in baking

Chervil – used in soups, salads, vinegars and garnish

Good King Henry – an early spinach-like crop

Lime mint – for summer drinks

Lovage – to flavour soups and casseroles

Sorrel – makes a wonderful sauce

GOOD ENOUGH TO EAT

Ciarán and Kealin Beattie supply chemical-free, locally grown flowers to businesses around Ireland through their company Leitrim Flowers. Their violas, pansies, cornflower, fuchsia, calendula and nasturtiums put a gorgeous finishing touch on dishes – a real feast for the eyes.

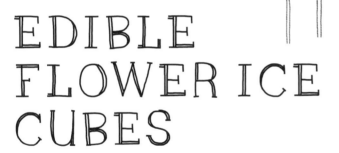

EDIBLE FLOWER ICE CUBES

MAKES 12 EXTRA LARGE CUBES

- Water (distilled water gives a really good effect)
- 2 extra large ice cube trays (we use silicone ice trays that make 6 cubes and are designed for sipping bourbon)
- 12 edible flowers in a variety of colours and shapes (source flowers that are grown to be eaten, without pesticides or other chemicals)

1 Although this seems a little time consuming, it's worth doing, as this process ensures the flowers are suspended perfectly in the cubes.
2 Fill ice cube trays about 1/3 full with water and add a flower (the flower should ideally be facing down). Freeze.
3 Once frozen, fill 2/3 full with water. Freeze.
4 Fill to the top with water and freeze again.

These look amazing in vintage cocktail glasses as part of an aperitif when guests arrive. For a really personal touch, ask your guests their favourite colour and use that to choose the right flower cube. What I love most about this is the ability to preserve the flowers a little longer than normal and to enjoy their beauty.

EDIBLE FLOWER SALAD WITH LEMON THYME DRESSING AND CRISPY PROSCIUTTO

We love nasturtiums and borage, lightly rinsed and patted dry. We grow a vivid red nasturtium which is more rare than the familiar orange ones, but so easy to grow. These give an amazing pop of colour on the plate.

SERVES 6

- 6 thinly sliced pieces of prosciutto
- 180ml (¾ cup) vegetable oil
- 120ml (½ cup) rice vinegar
- Juice and zest of two lemons
- 1 tablespoon thyme leaves
- ¼ teaspoon salt
- ¼ teaspoon freshly ground black pepper
- 300g (8 cups) spring leaves, rinsed and dried
- 100g (2 cups) edible flowers
- 100g (2 cups) soft goat's cheese
- 1 tablespoon bean sprouts

1 Preheat oven to 190C/375F.
2 Line a baking sheet with parchment paper and place prosciutto on it in a single layer. Bake until crisp, about 15 minutes. Allow to cool.
3 In a jar with a lid, add the oil, vinegar, lemon zest, lemon juice, thyme leaves, salt and pepper. Shake well.
4 To serve, divide salad greens and edible flowers among six chilled plates. Spoon dressing over and top with crispy prosciutto, sprouts and cheese.

BEST
FOOT
FORWARD

Getting out in nature is often reward in itself, but it can also be fun to have a goal to guide your ramblings. We often find ourselves gazing at the sky and into the sea. Here are the perennial favourites we watch out for on our scavenger hunts.

FEATHERED FRIENDS

The life of the twitcher might seem a bit uncool, but there's more to it than wearing tweed. Birdwatching has gone high-tech, and there are great smartphone apps out there - some that don't even require an internet connection to work. You get maps, photos, illustrations and samples of birdsong to make identification easy.

PERIWINKLES

Collecting these little guys is so much fun and it puts a new spin on a seaside walk. First make sure you're in a clean water area and check the state of the tide - high tide is generally not suitable. These blue-purpley snails are often easy to find clinging to the sides of rock pools and under the low tide boulders. Whelks, limpets, mussels and sea urchins are other creatures that can be harvested for eating if you want to have a go.

BEACHCOMBING BOOTY

We're always on the lookout for flotsam and jetsam to work into our living space. Nets, lobster pots and buoys make fun props for outdoor parties where you're serving fish and downing fruity rum cocktails. A great shell makes the perfect soap dish for the outdoor shower, while driftwood with weird rusty bits sticking out is instant art. In non-coastal parts of the world this is called litter-picking - but if you're by the sea it can become addictive.

CRAB CAKES

Crab is healthy, sustainable, tasty and eaten around the world – steamed, boiled or fried. My favourite are these coconut Thai crab cakes with sweet chilli ginger sauce. Yum!

SERVE 4 TO 6

- 450g (1 lb) white crabmeat (drained well to squeeze out any juice)
- 3 eggs or 2 large eggs
- 160g (1¼ cups) breadcrumbs, blended until fine
- 100g (1 cup) dried desiccated coconut
- 2 tablespoons soy sauce
- 2 tablespoons fish sauce
- 1 lime, zested and juiced
- 3 lime leaves, chopped, or 1 stalk of lemongrass, thinly sliced (often you'll find these frozen in Asian stores)
- 1 tablespoon ginger, grated
- 1 small red chilli
- 1 clove garlic
- 3 scallions (green onions), chopped
- Coriander, chopped
- Flour for coating
- Oil for light frying (vegetable is best)

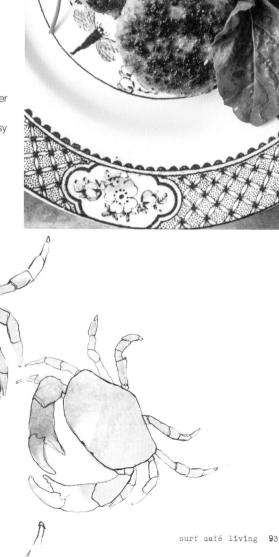

1 Halve the breadcrumbs and blend in a food processor with all the other ingredients. Blend until it forms a maleable consistency. If it's still too soft keep adding the breadcrumbs until the consistency becomes easy to form small round cakes, about the size of a golf ball.
2 Make the cakes, place on a tray and pat them flat. Allow them to firm up in the fridge for an hour or so. When ready to cook lightly coat in flour and shallow fry until golden.
3 Serve while warm with sweet chilli dipping sauce on the side. These also go well with Asian pickled vegetable salad and a glass of cool Chardonnay.

HERBY BUTTERY CRAB CLAWS

Prepared crabmeat can be expensive, but crab claws are generally cheaper and more fun to eat. They can be bought pre-cooked with half the shell removed, but if your fisherman friend has given you a big bag of claws, just pop them into some salted boiling water for a few minutes, rinse and allow to cool. Give the shell a good crack with a meat hammer or rolling pin so they are easier to eat. Don't forget to let your guests do some of this, as that's part of the fun of eating crab claws.

SERVES 2

- 2 small onions, finely diced
- 1 fennel, thinly sliced
- 2 tablespoons butter
- 100ml (¼ cup) white wine
- 2 tablespoons parsley and dill, chopped (fennel ends can also be used)
- 16 crab claws
- Salt and pepper
- 1 tablespoon tomato puree
- 1 teaspoon sugar
- A splash of olive oil
- Lemon, to decorate

1 Put a large pot straight onto the gas, splash in some oil and sweat off the diced onions. Pour in the wine and sliced fennel, then stir. Reduce right down so that there's hardly any liquid left. Next stir in the tomato puree. Slowly add the butter in stages, stirring through. Now add the crab claws.

2 Give a good stir and cook for 5 to 10 minutes. Keeping the lid on helps keep the moisture in but you will still need to stir occasionally. Add some seasoning – you may need the sugar depending on how sweet the fennel is, so make sure to taste before you season.

3 Once the claws are heated right through, sprinkle in the fresh herbs and stir (keeping back some dill for decoration at the plating up stage). If you like a little spice then throw in some Tabasco now.

4 Place the crab claws on a plate and top with dill and lemon. Sprinkle some sauce around the plate and serve with crusty bread. This is a great starter or also fab as a tapas style plate while sipping wine with friends. As a main course, serve with some herby homemade chips and fresh peas.

5 Chardonnay is a great wine with crab.

6 This dish forces you to get your hands messy and get involved with your food, so feel free to dish out bibs for a laugh.

SUSTAINABLE FISH... THE ONLY WAY FORWARD

Sustainable fish are fish that are harvested at a sustainable rate, where the fish population does not decline over time because of bad fishing practices.

Illegal fishing, over fishing, overexploitation, massive bycatch, too many boats in one area, pirate fishing and targeting specific fish like tuna or cod have led to mass decimation of global stocks. The only way to change this is to change our seafood eating habits, support better practices of fishing, eat fish that have a low bycatch (the other poor animals that get stuck in the nets), have stricter quotas on overfished species, and through educating people.

Have a think about it next time you are at the chippy and say no to cod and yes to pollock, hake or something that you have never heard of!

LET'S HELP

The cod, tuna, halibut and wild salmon.

let's munch down

Squid, mussels, crab and organic farmed fish.

WE DON'T LIKE

Gillnetting, purse seining, trawls and dredges

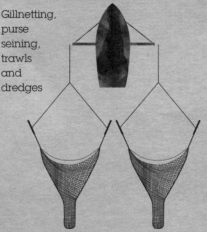

WE DO LIKE

Pole, line and troll fishing with lower bycatch and leaving some fish behind to grow a little bigger.

WHY WE LOVE SQUID

Who doesn't love deep-fried calamari? It's fantastic dipped into a little lemon mayonnaise, and only takes seconds to cook too.

Squid is tasty, easy to prepare, economical and most of all sustainable. It's an ocean-friendly choice for seafood lovers because it's a fast growing species and has a low rate of by-catch (when other fish get caught in the nets).

It's easily bought prepared and frozen, but you can't beat it fresh. It's easy to clean, so don't be afraid, and it's quite a cool skill to master too.

Here are my tips on how to prepare fresh calamari...

1 Spread out the calamari nice and straight. Gently separate the head with tentacles from the main body tube. You do this by pulling (not cutting) – hold on just below the eye and separate.

2 You now have a separate body (or tube) and head (with the tentacles). Hopefully the innards are still attached. If they aren't attached, squeeze the main body like an empty tube of toothpaste and all the innards should flow out.

3 Remove the dark spotty layer of skin on the tube; this is actually edible, but it looks better without. Now thoroughly wash out the inside. Use cold water for this, as hot water will start to partially cook the fish.

4 Using your fingers, pull out the plastic-like cartilage piece.

5 Alternatively, you can turn it inside out by pushing the tube on the back of a chopstick.

6 The tube is now clean and white.

7 Back to the head and the tentacles: cut away just under the eye and discard the innards. (At this point you can remove the squid ink sac for gourmet cooking if you want.)

8 The tentacles are completely edible and are best flash fried or cooked in a nice fishy soup.

9 Remove the 'beak' by squeezing the connective tissue at the top of the tentacle and it should easily pop out.

10 Rinse everything in cold running water and pat dry.

11 Calamari freezes well and thaws out easily.

12 Enjoy!

(TRY OUR CALAMARI RECIPES ON PAGE 48 AND 52)

SKATE YOUR WAY AROUND THIS RECIPE

Another great sustainable fish. Don't be afraid of this unusual looking creature – it's cheap, easy to cook and delish! Skate is always cooked on the bone (well, it's cartilage actually).

SERVES 2

- 2 skate wings, skinned and prepped (cut to size by the fishmonger)
- 50g (½ cup) flour, seasoned with black pepper
- 100g (½ cup) butter
- 1 lemon
- 3 tablespoons capers
- 1 tablespoon oil

1 Heat a large frying pan on a high heat and add the oil for frying.
2 Meanwhile dredge the fish wing in the seasoned flour, place the fish into the pan and start the cooking. Add half the butter to the pan and lower the heat.
3 Allow the fish to cook for 2 to 3 minutes on each side. Set aside when done. (Remember the fish keeps cooking in its own heat.)
4 Turn up the heat again and add the rest of the butter. Let it sizzle to a nice nutty colour and add the capers and a squeeze of lemon. Fry for 30 seconds.
5 Now pour the buttery juices over the fish and serve.
6 Serve with potato gratin, blanched greens and a crisp Riesling!

SEE FISH
AND EAT IT

Whenever there's a lack of summer surf, we find it's a perfect time to address our taste for fresh fish. Daryl Eweing runs mackerel fishing trips from Rosses Point, giving us a chance to cast our lines and see what we can pull up. Daryl says most people leave their catch with him because they don't know what to do with it – which seems a bit crazy! So here are two ideas of how to use your freshly-caught and gutted fish.

FRY IN A FLASH

1 First butterfly the mackerel, which means opening it up so it's all flat. Get a nice sizzling pan going with a thin layer of hot oil. (Don't use olive oil, as its smoke point is too low.) Place the mackerel skin down on the griddle for a solid two minutes.
2 While it's sizzling away, sprinkle on some salt and pepper. Take a look at the flesh; when it starts to change colour you'll know it's cooking through. At this point, flip it over with a long, thin spatula and allow it to cook flesh side down for 30 to 60 seconds. Rest it on kitchen paper for a minute, then plate up.

TIP: The pan must be sizzling all the time. If you got no sizzle, it ain't gonna work!

FISHY CURE

1 There are dry and wet methods of curing fish. The dry method is quite easy. For trout or salmon, you would make a blend of 50% salt and 50% sugar with a scattering of herbs – dill is the most common. For mackerel though, all you need is salt.
2 You'll need one fish made up of two fillets with the skin still on. Spread enough of the curing medium onto one fillet to yield a layer up to 1/2cm (1/4 inch) thick. Put the other fillet on top to make a kind of sandwich. Place a plate on top of the fish and weight this down. Keep it in the fridge, periodically pouring off the excess liquid. Mackerel is ready in two days – just rinse off the salt. Larger fish will need about three days. Cured fish is best served in nice, thin slices.

TIP: A milk jug or – better yet – a bottle of Champagne, makes a good weight.

BOARD MEETING

Stand-up paddleboarding is a great group activity because just about anybody can do it. Surfers use it as a way to maintain core stability when the waves have gone flat, and it's something most non-surfers pick up really easily.

Want to give it a try? It's worth booking a lesson so you get the most out of the experience. You can tailor your skills to the body of water you'll be paddling on – ocean, river or lake. Once you've got the basics, follow this checklist to create your own SUP adventure.

(1) Check the weather forecast – including wind speed, wind direction and both water and air temperature. You can always look at the trees and clouds to get an idea of how strong the wind is and which way it's blowing.

(2) Dress for the occasion – based on the weather report. You might need a wetsuit, gloves, boots and a hood – or you might find yourself needing nothing more than boardshorts and a cap.

(3) Look at the local webcams – so you know what to expect on the day. If the conditions look beyond your abilities, you might save yourself a fruitless drive.

(4) Know the tides – and how they fit with your plan.

This will give you an idea of how far you'll need to carry your board to the ocean's edge and whether to expect a shoredump on your entrance or exit from the sea.

(5) Pack some supplies – depending on how long you'll be out on the water. For example in summer you might take along water, an energy bar, a hat with a brim, sunblock and sunglasses.

(6) Prepare to get wet – because let's be frank – falling off is half the fun! If you bring a camera, you'll want a waterproof one. Invest in a waterproof pouch if you want your mobile to survive the trip. Finally, sunglasses might last longer worn on a strap.

STRANDHILL CHILL

Keep cool and caffeinated with these great iced coffee tips!

ICED COFFEE
- Fill a large glass with ice.
- Add a double shot of espresso.
- Top with cold water.

THE SHELLS FRAPPUCCINO
- Fill glass with ice three-quarters full. Put ice in blender. Add two scoops of vanilla ice cream, a double shot of espresso and milk. Blend.
- Top with a straw and chocolate sprinkles.
- Deluxe: add whipped cream to serve.

ICED LATTE
- Fill a large glass with ice.
- Add a double shot of espresso.
- Add flavour syrup: vanilla, caramel or hazlenut.
- Top with milk.

SEASIDE COOKIES

- 225g (1 cup) butter, softened
- 110g (½ cup) caster sugar
- 275g (1¾ cup) plain flour
- Ground spices or finely grated zest

1 Preheat oven to 180C/350F.
2 Cream the butter in a large bowl or in a food mixer until soft. Add the sugar and beat until the mixture is light and fluffy.
3 Sift in the flour and spices or zest and bring the mixture together to form a dough.
4 Roll out the dough, cut out shapes, place on a baking tray and bake for 13 to 15 minutes or until light golden brown.
5 Carefully transfer to a wire rack to cool.

TO ICE THE BISCUITS:

1 Make a batch of royal icing (below), divide into batches and colour accordingly. Fill piping bags fitted with small, plain nozzles with the icing.
2 You are now ready to unleash your creative side!
3 If flooding cookies (below) – pipe around the outline and leave to dry completely. Add some water to the remaining royal icing so it is runny, then fill a piping bag. Fill in the outline and then leave to dry.
4 Give these biscuits as a present to friends and family or simply revel in your fabulousness while enjoying the finished products.

ROYAL ICING MADE SIMPLE

- 3 tablespoons meringue powder
- 450g (4 cups) icing sugar
- 5-6 tablespoons warm water

1 Beat all ingredients in a mixer until the icing forms peaks (7 to 10 minutes at a low speed with a heavy duty mixer, 10 to 12 minutes at high speed with a hand-held mixer).
2 Keep all utensils completely grease-free for proper icing consistency.
3 Flooding cookies means that you pipe a continuous outline on the cookies then leave it to dry. When it's dried you then fill in the space with a runnier icing and ideally leave to dry overnight. You can create all different types of patterns this way and it's easy and effective.
4 For flooding cookies, thin a small portion of the royal icing by adding ½ teaspoon of water and mixing with a spatula until you reach a runny honey consistency. If you add too much water then don't worry just add some of the thicker royal icing to it!
5 Colouring royal icing is easy. I find the colour gels and pastes far easier to use and you only need a tiny amount. I always use a cocktail stick dipped into the paste and then transfer to the royal icing a little at a time. Mix well to achieve the desired colour.
6 Keep all of your royal icing covered so it doesn't dry out. If this happens then you will have to re-beat the mixture to get rid of any lumps.

AUTUM

SWEETEN THE DEAL

We first met Mary from Mill Lane Honey when she dropped off a sample of her honey to sell in Shells Little Shop. As soon as we tasted it we were hooked: Sweet, gooey, pure and most importantly, 100% local. We literally can't keep it on the shelf in our shop. That, for me, is the best seal of approval. Here's what Mary has to say about bee keeping.

"My dad kept bees when I was a teenager, but I had absolutely no interest whatsoever. But in 2005 I got interested in self-sufficiency and producing my own food. From two polytunnels I started growing salad and vegetables for local markets. I'm not quite sure what little worm got into my head, but I started to think about keeping bees. I spent a week at the Federation of Irish Beekeeping Associations' summer school and came out of it with my preliminary standard certificate at the end.

At Mill Lane Honey, we have our own bees and also a network of beekeeping friends. I have a supplier in Sligo, and that's what we sell at Shells Café in Strandhill. The more local the honey, the better for any kind of ailment, especially allergic reactions involving pollen. It works like a vaccination; the pollens in local honey build up immunity in your system.

I use our honey in homemade granola, and I love to drizzle it on anything with cooked goat's cheese in it. It's very whimsical to be perfectly honest! It's a bit like salt in my kitchen – it's there by the cooker and on the table all the time."

"I will arise and go now, and go to Innisfree,
And a small cabin build there, of clay and wattles made:
Nine bean-rows will I have there, a hive for the honey-bee,
And live alone in a bee-loud glade."

- From The Lake Isle of Innisfree by WB Yeats

TOP PLANTS FOR BEES

Whether you raise honeybees or not, cultivate these plants to help keep the world's pollinators happy...

- Apple
- Bluebell
- Borage
- Bramble
- Heather
- Honeysuckle
- Lavender
- Marjoram
- Pussy willow
- Red clover
- Rosemary
- Sunflower
- Sweet pea
- Thyme

WANT TO GET BUSY KEEPING BEES AND HARVESTING YOUR OWN HONEY?

Here are some key facts to get you started...
) A healthy hive produces an average of **20kg (44lbs) of honey** a year.
) To forage, bees may fly up to **3 miles.**
) Beehives normally measure **two feet square** or less.
) As many as **80,000 bees** make up a typical colony in the height of summer.
) Bees pollinate **75%** of our most vital crops and fave foods.
) There are an estimated **24,000 beehives** in Ireland.

The minimum tools you'll need include...
) Protective clothing – a light coloured bee suit, gloves and boots to cover the ankles.
) A smoker – a canister with a bellows that creates smoke, essential to keeping bees under control.
) Hive tool – to separate your frames and clean excess wax and propolis.
) A hive – which you can buy commercially or even make yourself.

HOMEMADE PEANUT BUTTER
ON TOAST WITH HONEYCOMB

Sometimes it's the simple things in life that you need. Peanut butter on toast with honey is one of those things. Here we show you how to make the best slice you will ever have.

- 450g (4 cups) unsalted peanuts (skinned and roasted)
- 2 tablespoons groundnut oil, or peanut oil if you have some
- 1 teaspoon salt
- 1 tablespoon honey (if you have a sweet tooth)

1 Place the peanuts, salt and honey (if you are using it) into a food processor, blitz for a couple of minutes and slowly drizzle the oil in until you have a smooth consistency. Taste and season accordingly, adding more salt if you like.

2 There you go, job done!

3 Place the peanut butter into an airtight container and store in the refrigerator. This should last a couple of months but no doubt you will finish it before then.

4 The oil will separate, so just stir it through next time you use it.

5 The next step is to get some thick cut toast on the go. Make sure it's proper good bread and not factory mass produced stuff. Respect the honey!

6 Smoother with peanut butter and drizzle with natural honey. We have used natural honeycomb made by little Irish black bees.

HHHMMMMM...
HONEY LOAF

Sometimes simple recipes are the best, if you like honey you will love honey loaf

- 710g/6oz of honey
- 140g/5oz of butter
- 85g/3oz of brown sugar
- 200g/7oz self-raising flour
- 2 eggs
- Tablespoon of water
  |For the icing
- 85g/3oz icing sugar
- 2 tablespoons of honey
- Juice of half a lemon
- 1 tablespoon of hot water
- 3 tablespoon of toasted flaked almond
  (optional)

1 Preheat oven to 180C/350F/Gas 3 and line your loaf tin with a layer of oil or butter then baking parchment so it sits neatly.

2 In a small pot, gently melt the butter, sugar, honey and water together.

3 Grab a cake bowl, sift the flour and break in the eggs and add the melted liquid. Quickly stir the ingredients together to form a cake batter but do not over work the batter.

4 Spoon into your loaf tin and bake for around 50 minutes. To test to see if the loaf is fully baked, insert a knife into the middle of the loaf, draw out, the loaf is baked if there is no wet batter mix lined on the knife , the knife should run clear, if it is not, then allow for a further ten minutes baking and test again.

5 Cool slightly in the tin before turning out onto a wire rack.

6 While the loaf is still warm, make the icing by mixing the icing sugar and honey together with the lemon juice and hot water. Grab a skewer and poke a few holes into the loaf. Spoon over the loaf as desired, trickling down the skewered holes, wait for icing to cool a little and add more icing to build up layers.

7 If you like, scatter toasted flaked almonds on top.

8 Try the honey loaf with a nice strong cup of Assam tea, picking away with dates and bananas.

KOEKSISTERS
(PLAITED DOUGH CAKES)

These are like super-sweet doughnuts, very popular back home. I grew up on these bad boys and the minute I land back in Cape Town I go to my favourite milk bar and tuck in. It's a super energy rush after tackling some big autumn swells too.

DOUGH
- 480g (4 cups) plain flour
- 5 teaspoons baking powder
- 1 teaspoon salt
- 125g (½ cup) butter
- 375ml (1½ cups) iced water

SYRUP
- 800g (4 cups) sugar
- 375ml (1½ cups) iced water
- 1 tablespoon golden syrup/honey
- Pinch of cream of tartar
- Juice of one lemon

FOR THE SYRUP
1 Mix all the ingredients and slowly heat until the sugar has dissolved. Boil for two to three minutes. Leave to cool, and store the syrup in the fridge or freezer until it is needed.

TO MAKE THE KOEKSISTER
1 Sift the dry ingredients, rub in the butter and mix in the iced water to make a soft dough.
2 Roll out to a thickness of 1cm (half an inch). Cut the dough in strips and plait.
3 Deep fry in vegetable oil at 165°C until golden brown, remove and dip immediately in ice-cold syrup. TIP: The oil must not be too hot, or the koeksisters will brown too quickly on the outside while remaining raw on the inside. Serve cold and remember to dollop with fresh honey. Delish.

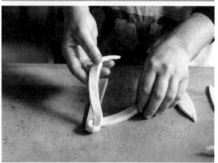

SMOKY BUTTER BEANS AND CHORIZO ON TOAST

Like baked beans? Well, this recipe is like pimped-up baked beans on toast. Butter beans baby!

SERVES 2 TO 4

- 2 tins butter beans (cannellini can be used too), drained
- 1 onion, finely chopped
- 2 tablespoons tomato puree
- 1 tin chopped tomato
- Dash of olive oil
- 3 cloves garlic, finely chopped
- 2 heaped teaspoons smoked paprika
- 1 de-seeded chilli, finely chopped
- 1 teaspoon allspice/pimento spice
- ½ teaspoon cayenne pepper
- Salt and pepper to season
- Fresh flat leaf parsley
- ½ lemon, zested
- 2 tablespoons sugar
- 4 slices buttered crusty toast

1 Begin with sweating off the diced onions and garlic in a heavy saucepan with some olive oil. Once things start browning through, throw in the spices and chilli, holding back the sugar. Gently stir. The onions should be coated with a nice reddish colour and the oil should have a good flavour. At this stage keep an eye on the heat, as you may need to turn it down a bit.

2 Pour in the drained butter beans, stir in the tomato puree and allow to cook for a minute, then add the tin of chopped tomato. Stir and allow to simmer for 5 to 10 minutes. Add in the sugar, reducing down the liquid. Taste and season.

3 Serve onto hot buttered toast, sprinkling on chopped flat leaf parsley, the zest of a lemon and a drizzle of olive oil. If you're feeling adventurous add a poached egg on top.

4 Tuck in.

HOME ALONE BANANA PANCAKES

Don't wait until you have people over or are entertaining. This is a foolproof, quick, easy and tasty pancake recipe for ONE. It was given to us by our mad Swedish friend, Anna Klara. She travels a lot and stays in random houses, hostels and on couches... so she finds this great for keeping up her energy through the day. So treat yourself when you're chilling solo.

MAKES 2-3 PANCAKES
- 1 cup flour
- 1 banana, ripe
- 1 egg
- 1 teaspoon ground cardamom
- Vegetable oil to fry

TO SERVE:
- Crème fraîche
- Whipped cream and berries
- Drizzle of honey

1 Mix the flour, banana and egg in a bowl. Add the cardamom.
2 Fry in a pan over not too high a heat.
3 The only way this will fail is if you burn them. Remember to keep them small; these are supposed to be mini-pancakes (about the size of the palm of your hand) so you can pop them in your mouth and not even bother with a knife or fork.

CLIP
AND
COLLECT

A mood board approach to installing art and prints really suits our style. We like to chop and change, introducing new inspirations all the time. Here are some guidelines for working with this kind of look.

One easy idea is to select pieces that all share the same colour palette.

Or, group images by subject matter – for example, lots of different pictures in a maritime theme.

Another tip is to gather eclectic images but create unity by using identical or similar frames.

Lots of work by one artist in different sizes, media and frames creates a cool look.

For temporary hanging solutions, use Blu-Tac, small clips, Washi tape (decorative masking tape) or clothes pegs.

Create visual interest by varying sizes, shapes and angles.

Quirky frames can contain wallpaper, wrapping paper or postcards stuck directly on the wall.

Showcase tea towels and fabric swatches as well as cards, labels and typography.

If you're not keen on holes in your wall or live in rented accommodation, stack pieces against the wall on the floor or on a shelf.

In a kitchen, consider heat, steam and splashes – this is a good room for chalkboard paint and disposable imagery.

Some walls are just too big or dramatic for this loose, scattered look. In which case, go big! Because the wall behind our sofa unit faces out to Knocknarea, we knew a piece with real wow factor was needed, so we commissioned a massive canvas from Sligo artist Andrea Flanagan.

CUSTOM CUPS

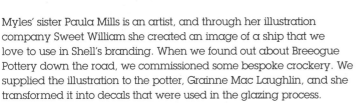

Myles' sister Paula Mills is an artist, and through her illustration company Sweet William she created an image of a ship that we love to use in Shell's branding. When we found out about Breeogue Pottery down the road, we commissioned some bespoke crockery. We supplied the illustration to the potter, Grainne Mac Laughlin, and she transformed it into decals that were used in the glazing process.

Voilà – our mugs feature the illustration and really evoke Strandhill. If you know of a local craftsperson, ask about minimum production runs and the possibility of commissioning unusual pieces to celebrate your own space.

SPICED BUTTERNUT SQUASH SOUP

This is one of our best-selling soups in the café and a favourite to serve for lunch at home with freshly baked bread. Butternut is that weird looking pumpkin thing that a lot of people ignore in the shops. It's cheap, tasty and versatile. Roasted, smashed or made into a soup, butternut is easy to cook and delicious.

SERVES 4 TO 6
- 1 large butternut, peeled, deseeded and diced
- 2 onions, diced
- 1 thumb-size piece of ginger, grated
- 3 cloves garlic, diced
- 2 tins chopped tomato
- 1 tablespoon tomato puree
- 2 heaped teaspoons cumin powder
- 1 teaspoon smoked paprika
- 1 tablespoon cumin seeds
- 1 teaspoon turmeric
- ½ teaspoon cayenne pepper (more if you like it spicy)
- 2 tablespoons sugar
- Salt and pepper
- 50ml (¼ cup) cream
- 75g (⅓ cup) butter
- Splash of vegetable oil
- 700-1000ml (approx 3 cups) stock

TO SERVE
- Crème fraîche
- Toasted pumpkin seeds
- Sprinkle of cayenne/smoked paprika

1 Grab a deep pot, pop it on the hob and heat up a splash of oil to get things going.
2 Toss in the cumin seed to flavour the oil. Allow to mingle for a minute.
3 Next sauté the garlic, ginger and onions for a few minutes.
4 Perhaps another splash of oil is needed now.
5 Add the squash and carrots and let them sweat it out for around 4 minutes on a high heat stirring occasionally.
6 Add in a tablespoon of tomato puree.
7 Cook for a further minute, stirring hard and covering the vegetables in the red paste.
8 Next add the two tins of chopped tomato, cumin, turmeric, cayenne and paprika to the mix. Stir it all together.
9 Cover the vegetables with a good stock, somewhere between 700-1000ml (4 cups) of stock. Let the soup simmer away for around 45 minutes, checking the water level every now and then.
10 Take off the heat and blend with a stick blender or food processor. While blending, add in the cream and butter. Butter will help to get a smooth shiny texture.
11 Salt and pepper, taste and season accordingly. Add some cracked black pepper on top. If you are doing this during the festive season, it's super nice to add some nutmeg as well.
12 Serve in bowls with a spoon of crème fraîche, pan toasted pumpkin seeds and a sprinkle of cayenne or paprika.

IN PRAISE OF PICKLES

TUCKING INTO YOUR HOME MADE PICKLES A FEW WEEKS AFTER MAKING THEM IS VERY REWARDING. A GREAT WAY TO USE UP EXTRA VEG.

HOW TO SERVE:

❭ Sharp pickles should accompany hard cheeses. The sharpness of vinegary gherkins for instance balances nicely with the bite of an aged cheddar.

❭ Strong, soft cheeses really need sweeter flavours like fresh fruit to cut into that tang of ammonia.

❭ Like a dry Martini, a dry goat's cheese goes well with little pickled pearl onions.

❭ Mediterranean pickled peppers go great with soft, salty cheeses.

❭ Pickles are incredibly healthy, and they make a gorgeous mid-afternoon snack.

❭ For pre-dinner, pickled mushrooms are popular in some parts of Europe and make a terrific complement to sliced meats.

❭ Fresh pickling is a quick way to enhance a vegetable's flavour that lasts a few days rather than several months. Mix one part water, one part vinegar, salt and sugar to taste, then throw in slices of any vegetable that you've got in abundance into a jar.

❭ Asian pickles come in fantastic colours and add a punch to plates. Pickled pink ginger is a favourite in our house.

❭ Historically, in some cultures they would drink a little shot of vinegar each morning for health. So when you run out of a favourite pickle but are left with the brine, you could always throw a little glass back.

TOASTED SESAME AND CORIANDER CREAM CHEESE

If there's one recipe you must try from this book it's this one! So far I have yet to find a person who does not like this dip. This is the mother of all dips, totally dipilicious.

MAKES A LARGE BOWLFUL

- 400g (16oz) full fat cream cheese
- 4 tablespoons toasted sesame seeds (just toast lightly in a hot pan)
- 2 tablespoons toasted sesame oil
- 1 large bunch coriander, de-stalked and chopped roughly
- 3 tablespoons sweet chilli sauce
- 3 twists black pepper
- 1 pinch salt

1 In a large bowl combine all the ingredients together. I find stirring it all in with a fork is better. Scoop out into a nice serving bowl and dip away.
2 If you have some left over, this is also amazing on a bacon toasty the next day, topped with a fried egg.

TREASURE
IN THE TREES

One of my favourite times to walk is in the autumn, when the air is fresh and there's so much colour and change everywhere. Now that we have Milkshake the mad dog, we try to vary our walks and often hit the woods, where she can run free (and get lost in the bushes) while we gather beautiful branches for floral arrangements, and berries and cobnuts for baking.

We've even latched onto the geocaching trend – if you haven't tried it, give it a go. It's basically a global treasure hunt; you get a clue and sat nav directions, and when you find the spot there's a little logbook and treasure. Checkout the website, www.geocaching.com, which lists all geocaching sites. It's a fantastic way to discover new walks in the area, but remember to bring a little gift to replace the one you find. Have fun!

BERRY NICE

...So, what can you do with all your foraged berries?

- Gently heat them up with a little bit of sugar and lemon juice until they breakdown a little, cool, and then stir them into your favourite Greek yoghurt.
- Turn them into jam, by boiling equal amounts of sugar and berries (i.e.1 kg of berries to 1 kg of sugar), cook for at least 25 minutes and spoon into hot jam jars while the jam is still piping hot. Enjoy on a Sunday afternoon with tea and homemade scones.
- Wash and scatter on a lovely salad with soft goat's cheese and mixed baby leaves.
- Add some pan roasted nuts and a sharp, sweet dressing.
- Decorate the top of your favourite cake with your own foraged berries – the perfect excuse to get baking! I find a rich chocolate cake with berry topping goes down a treat.
- Making an apple crumble? Why not make it an apple blackberry crumble?
- Foraged berry smoothie – add a banana and some yoghurt for a delicious, healthy start to the day
- Scatter blackberries on your granola, or better yet fold them into our lovely Bircher muesli recipe on page 33
- Mash up berries that are a bit bruised and not so fresh with a fork, then add them to a simple salad dressing: Pop a handful of mashed berries, 5 tablespoons of olive oil, 3 tablespoons of red wine vinegar, 1 tablespoon of sugar and a pinch of cracked black pepper into a jam jar and shake hard for a quick, easy homemade dressing.
- It is all berry, berry simple!

BLACKBERRY MARTINI!

Mash your berries with a fork, scoop into a cocktail shaker and add vodka, pineapple juice and ice, then shake hard. Pour into Martini glasses and garnish with a berry.

HALLOWEEN
FANCY DRESS SURF SESSION

We all love a good excuse for fancy dress, so we decided to pull off the Shells Halloween Surf Session, which everyone in the village could be part of. You didn't even have to be able to surf to get involved… The prizes were all about the costume, the fun and whether you made it back out of the water in full costume. It's a great way to get everyone in the sea for the start of winter, too. All the surf schools lent us foamy boards and the Sligo Surf Club organised an amp and speaker, so we had great running commentary and music. Shells kept everyone warm with coffees and prizes. I would also recommend a sneaky flask of whiskey for after the surf!

AUTUMN TABLE STYLING

Ideas for autumn tables

❯ Plant woody herbs like rosemary in vintage tins, or put them in clean soup tins and terracotta pots.

❯ Dip-dyeing looks really cool and is super-easy. Go for bold colours to lift plain containers and make a feature of your indoor herb garden. We used bright yellow on a terracotta pot.

❯ Break with tradition and look out for unusually shaped and coloured gourds, then group them together.

❯ Mini pumpkins can be sprayed a modern colour for a cooler twist.

❯ Cut a log into discs. Drip candlewax in the centre of one side of each 'plate', then squish a candle into the molten wax to hold it upright in place.

S P A R K S &
R E F L E C T I O N

Everything looks so romantic in low light, so after a busy day at Shells we like to create a nice atmosphere in the house by burning candles.

It's really easy to make your own. We have loads of candles left over from the supper clubs at Shells so we like to collect them up and get to work reviving the wax for future gatherings. Vintage junk can make really good containers – old tins, enamel jugs and pewter teapots all look amazing with candlelight.

❯ Don't mix scented with unscented or citronella candle wax

❯ Unless you want to end up with dirty brown candles, don't mix colours of wax

❯ Trim off all the soot and burnt wicks, digging into the wax to remove dirty bits

❯ Melt the wax in a double boiler (a bowl on top of a pan of simmering water)

❯ Fish out old wicks and other dirty stuff with wooden chopsticks

❯ Assemble your container, which must be super-clean

❯ Cut a piece of cotton string that's 10cm longer than the height of your vessel

❯ Dip this wick briefly in the wax to coat it

❯ Wrap one end of the wick around a chopstick

❯ Rest the chopstick across the mouth of the vessel with one end of the wick dangling

❯ Adjust so that the dangling end touches the bottom of the container

❯ If the container you're using has a bigger opening, then you can use a few wicks to create a cool look

❯ Pour wax into the container very slowly to prevent bubbles

❯ As the wax cools, the part around the wick might sink, so just fill this divot with more liquid wax

❯ When the wax cools, you've got a new candle!

ONION BREAD WITH ROSEMARY

Fresh warm bread, home baked, is really simple and has a lot of wow factor – especially if you do it the way I've outlined below. Be confident and give this a go. Bread is easier than you think.

MAKES 1 LARGE OR 2 SMALL LOAVES

- 450g (4 cups) strong bread flour
- 2 tablespoons olive/rapeseed oil
- 2 onions, finely chopped and dried in an oven for 15 to 25 minutes at 170C/340F
- 2 teaspoons fresh rosemary, chopped
- 2 teaspoons salt
- 30g (1oz) dried yeast
- 2 teaspoons sugar
- 250ml (1¼ cup) lukewarm water (not too hot or the yeast will die)

1. To begin, place the flour, oven-dried onions, oil, salt, sugar and rosemary into a mixing bowl.
2. In a separate small bowl, activate the dried yeast with a little of the warm water. Give it a couple of minutes, then add it into the dry mix together with the rest of the water.
3. Mix by hand into a sticky dough.
4. Remove the dough from the bowl and knead lightly on a floured surface.
5. Give your arms a good workout and knead the dough for a solid 10 minutes. You can make it easier by cutting the dough in two. Feel free to solicit the help of your kids or a friend, making it even more fun. It's a great way to involve your guests.
6. Place the well-kneaded dough into a large, lightly greased bowl. The bowl should be twice the size of the dough (alternatively use a large pot).
7. Cover with cling film and leave to prove in a nice warm spot until the dough has doubled in size (about 30 to 50 minutes).
8. Preheat oven to 200C/400F.
9. Turn out dough onto a lightly floured surface and gently knock back (knead roughly for a few minutes), then re-shape the dough into the size of your preferred baking container.
10. Now here's the fun part... Why not try some of these choices:
11. Bake in a clay pot for plants – looks super cool and rustic.
12. Bake in an old-school cast-iron pot with lid. We use an old Le Creuset pot. The lid creates an oven within an oven, resulting in a lovely crusty loaf of bread.
13. Bake in used tin cans. Divide the dough into two-thirds the size of the can you are using. Looks totally rad once baked. And you can have one per guest too – super cute and super special.
14. Last step, bake your bread at 200C/400F for around 30 to 35 minutes. Turn out onto a wire cooling rack and allow to cool before serving.

SPATCHCOCK CHICKEN WITH SALSA VERDE

Everyone loves a roast chicken; it's cheap, easy to do and a crowd pleaser.

SERVES 4 TO 6

Here's something a bit different to try next time you are roasting a chook: Spatchcock the chicken for a faster, easier and more even cooking process. Once it's cooked, you don't carve the chicken, instead serve each guest their favourite joint, or go for a quarter of the chicken per person.

1 Begin by turning the bird upside down – breast down, wings on top.
2 Either with a sharp knife, scissors or – even better – garden shears, start cutting just beside the backbone, cutting through the ribs and along, going front to back.
3 Start the second cut on the other side of the backbone and cut all the way though. This will make the backbone completely cut out.
4 Spread the bird open and turn over, pressing down until it is spread out relatively flat.
5 If you are feeling confident, try to remove the breast (keel) bone by snipping out along the cartilage of the breasts and slicing the bone in half.
6 At this point there are plenty of options. You can keep butchering until you have quartered the chicken, or roast it whole with lots of spices and rubs.
7 My favourite is to shove some herb flavoured butter under the skin and a generous rub of salt and herbs on the outside. Mortar and pestle the dried herbs and sea salt to make a good rub.
8 You can marinate the chicken in curry spices and yoghurt for 24 hours.
9 A salty brine marinade produces a wonderfully juicy chicken.
10 Roast the spatchcock bird on a wire rack at 200C/390F, catching all the juices below. Halfway through cooking use those juices to baste the chicken. Do this several times over for a crispy and flavourful chicken.
11 Serve with my crispy potatoes and zingy hand cut salsa verde.

SALSA VERDE

- Handful of roughly chopped parsley, coriander and basil
- 2 tablespoons chopped capers
- 4 anchovy fillets, chopped
- 1 clove garlic, grated
- Sea salt
- 100ml (½ cup) olive oil
- 1 small onion/shallot, finely chopped

Hand chop and mix in a bowl to make a vibrant green herby dressing. Don't skip the anchovies – they won't taste fishy but will deliver salty savoury goodness. Yum...

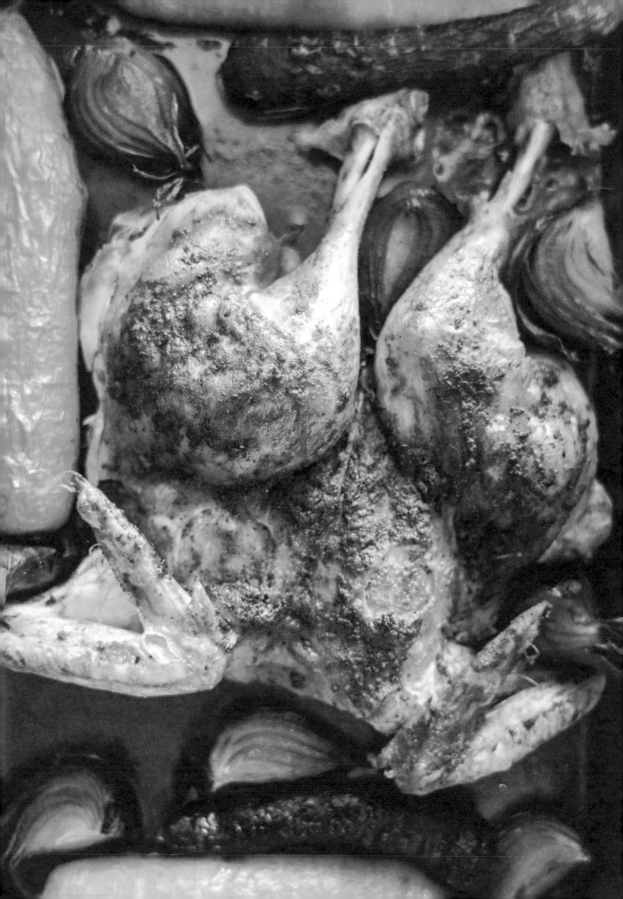

CHOCOLATE RASPBERRY TART

This oh so decadent dessert is perfect for late summer and early autumn, when raspberries are in season. The combination of bitter-sweet chocolate and tangy raspberries is without a doubt one of the best food combinations out there.

SERVES 8

1 Add the butter and whizz until it starts to look like fine breadcrumbs. Beat the egg yolk and water together. Add to the crumbly mixture and blitz until it all sticks together. This can also be done by hand but it takes a little more work. Turn out onto a surface dusted with flour and knead briefly until smooth. It should be a dark, chocolatey colour. Shape into a flat disc, wrap in cling film, then chill in the fridge for about half an hour.

2 Remove the pastry from the fridge and roll it out thinly on a flour-dusted surface. Use it to line a 25cm (10 inch diameter), 4cm (1½ inch) deep, loose-bottomed tart tin. Trim the pastry edges if you want (some pros do the trimming after the baking).

3 Put a baking sheet onto the middle shelf of the oven and preheat to 200C/390F. Line the pastry case with a sheet of crumpled baking paper and a thin layer of baking beans or rice, then blind bake on the preheated baking tray for 15 minutes. Remove the paper and beans/rice and blind bake for 5 more minutes. Blind baking is basically baking the pastry before filling it, using a weight to stop the pastry from rising in the middle.

4 Remove from the oven and leave to cool. Turn the oven down to 170C/340F.

BEGIN WITH MAKING THE PASTRY

- 175g (1¼ cups) plain flour, plus extra for dusting
- 30g (¼ cup) good quality cocoa powder
- 50g (⅖ cup) icing sugar
- 100g chilled butter, diced
- 1 medium egg yolk
- 4 teaspoons cold water

FOR THE FILLING, WHILE YOUR PASTRY BAKES:

- 150ml whole milk
- 500ml double cream
- 65g (⅓ cup) golden caster sugar
- 300g good quality dark chocolate (at least 70% cocoa solids), broken into small squares
- 2 medium free range eggs
- 1 teaspoon vanilla extract
- 250g fresh raspberries, plus extra to serve

NOW IT'S TIME FOR THE FILLING:

5 Put the milk, cream and sugar into a pan and slowly bring to a simmer, stirring gently. Take off the heat, add the chocolate squares and stir until smooth. Cool slightly for 5 minutes, then add the eggs and vanilla extract, and mix together well. You should now have a thick, shiny chocolate filling.

6 Scatter the raspberries in the tart case and slowly pour in the batter to cover all the raspberries… then lick the pot!

7 Pop the tart back into the cooled oven and bake for around 30 to 40 minutes, until baked with a slight wobble to the filling.

8 Cool for around an hour (not in the fridge), before serving with dusted raspberries and champagne – you deserve it after baking this one!

ALL CLEAR

We love collecting vintage glassware and get a real buzz in adding to the collection. It's such a cheap way to add flavour to a space and personality to a party.

> Funny, unusual shapes and styles will inspire you to serve something a bit different. For example, kitsch souvenir glasses demand fruity rum cocktails, go with an old-school cocktail in a champagne coupe, put port in 1970s liqueur glasses and get more life out of jam jars by filling them with short drinks and huge ice cubes.

> When you've got kids over, include them in the fun by letting them pick out their own glass, and be sure to have some colourful cordial on hand so they can feel a part of the mixed drink effort.

> We love the Moroccan tea glasses we bought on a trip a while back, and guests love the showmanship of mint tea served the North African way.

MINT TEA, REFRESHINGLY GOOD

Instead of serving coffee after dinner, try mint tea in vintage glasses as an alternative.

Fill one teapot with fresh mint and boiling water and have an empty teapot to hand. Pour the tea from one pot to another to aerate the drink, then distribute into glasses containing mint sprigs. A long pour from a significant height adds authenticity.

WINTER

MEET THE MAKER

Adrian from Sheerin's Meatin Place has been supplying us at the café for over three years now. When we're having dinner parties at home, he's the first person we call. Not only is he a craft butcher who sources all of his meat from our local area, but he's also a foodie – which is a great combination. We'll have a chat about what we want to do and he suggests the best cuts of the best meat, and gets it all ready for collection. I always recommend getting into a conversation with your butcher – they have so much knowledge that a small tip can transform your dinner.

"We've a long, long history – five generations of butchers. My father had a butchers shop before me and I'm using his premises. I'm nine years in business and started working with Myles when Shells Café opened. I would say that I'm every bit as passionate as he is about food.

"When I started I was 12 or 13. Believe it or not, I was slaughtering sheep and lambs. I didn't really like it because it was hard work at a very young age, and very physical as well. But it was good for me; I got a very good grounding in hard work. And I don't know any different! My brother is a great butcher and fantastic to work with. We have a very good work ethic.

What makes me happy? Just producing good food for good people. We take time, we don't rush it. You have to enjoy it as well. We try to have a nice atmosphere, maybe some music on in the background and just keep it chilled. We have very good, high quality meat. That is the secret of everything in life: put the best in. The proof of the pudding is in the eating."

BEEF & BEER MAN PIE!

So ladies, when you're tired of cooking all the time, show your man this recipe and tell him to tackle it like a true hero. I'm sure he will be up for the challenge. And men, if you're tired of doing all the cooking then ask your lady to cook you up a real man pie – she'll be delighted to feed you a big, hearty meal.

This recipe calls for suet. Now don't be put off by this strange fatty substance. It can be readily bought in most supermarkets – look for it in the baking aisle.

SERVES 4

You will need a food processor, an ovenproof casserole dish and a pie dish or large shallow bowl.

- 1 onion, diced
- 1 celery stick, chopped
- 2 carrots, peeled and chopped
- 3 or 4 small white onions or shallots kept whole
- 2 garlic cloves, diced
- 700g/1.5lb stewing beef, cubed
- 2 sprigs thyme
- 2 tablespoons olive oil
- 55g/2oz butter
- 1 tablespoon Bovril or beef stock cubes
- 2 tablespoons flour
- 1 tablespoon Worcester sauce
- 2 pints beer, dark and strong (that's one pint for the recipe and one to drink while cooking)
- 1 egg, beaten
- 1 teaspoon sesame or poppy seeds (optional)
- Salt and pepper

FOR THE PASTRY
- 500g/1.1lb plain flour
- 250g/9oz suet

1. Preheat the oven to 160C/320F.
2. Grab a nice heavy ovenproof casserole dish and begin your stew by sweating your onions and garlic in the olive oil.
3. Next add the beef and get it browning nicely on all sides.
4. Melt in the butter and then add the tablespoon of flour; stir hard and coat the meat in the thickening agent.
5. Quickly add your vegetables and thyme and keep stirring.
6. Next pour in the beer, the Bovril or beef stock cubes, Worcester sauce and some seasoning.
7. Once the stew has come together, pop it in the oven with the lid on for around three hours, taking off the lid in the last half hour to thicken up the sauce.
8. While this is happening get crackin' on with the pastry.
9. In a food processor, blitz together the suet and flour until there are no more lumpy suet bits – about three minutes – and then slowly add one tablespoon of water at a time until the pastry starts to come together to form a dough.
10. Turn out onto a floured surface and gently bring the pastry together with your hands. Do not overwork the pastry, as this will give it a chewy texture.
11. Roll out half your pastry and use it to line your dish and form the base of your pie.
12. Use a slotted spoon to scoop in your stewy mix (pouring it all in at once makes the pie too wet so it will leak everywhere). Top up the pie with some sauce to nicely coat everything. Keep the rest of the sauce for later when serving.
13. Roll out remaining pastry to cover the pie. Trim the edges, and then 'crimp' with a fork to seal everything up.
14. Brush the top of the pie with a beaten egg and scatter on a few sesame seeds or poppy seeds if you wish.
15. For effect, you can also use the excess trimmings to paste on leafy shapes or any shape you want. (I use a skull and crossbone cookie cutter!)
16. Bake for around 40 minutes until golden brown and crisp.
17. Let the pie rest for about ten minutes. Serve it up with herby mashed potato, peas and the extra sauce.
18. And a pint of beer, of course.

BRAISING

Long winter nights call for comfort food, with lots of slow-cooking. Big cheap cuts of meat are great cooked with a method called 'braising'. In braising, food is first seared (cooked quickly at a high temperature) and then simmered over a long time in a small amount of liquid. Braising is often done in a pot on the stove (as in a 'pot roast') but can also be done in the oven.

The general idea is to heat up the oven tray or cast iron pot on the stove and brown off a cheaper, tougher cut of meat from beef, pork or lamb in oil or fat. Add a liquid like wine or stock and reduce the liquid down a little, then seal the dish with foil or a tight fitting lid. Now slow cook away. A nice tip is to add the vegetables to cook with the meat.

For the best results I like to buy a cut of meat on the bone. The recipe I have chosen is beef short ribs, an unusual cut that might make your butcher raise an eyebrow. But most butchers will be happy to accommodate you and it will most likely be nice and cheap.

BRAISED SHORT RIBS

My favourite winter dish...

The short rib is an unusual cut of meat but very cheap and so delicious if cooked slowly. Your local butcher will have them in multi-rib strips, like a pork rack. Get your butcher to cut them into individual portions – two per person is plenty.

SERVES 4

- 8 short ribs
- 1 whole garlic bulb, crushed
- 1 bottle cheap red wine
- 200g (¾ cup) tomato puree
- Salt and pepper
- Fresh parsley, chopped
- 1 tablespoon sugar
- Glug of oil
- You will also need a thick roasting pan.

1 Begin on top of the hob, by browning each side of the meat joints with the oil. Throw in the crushed garlic, and allow to sizzle so all those yummy meat juices are released.

2 Spoon in the tomato puree and sugar. Stir around, coating the pan and the meat in the red sauce. Next add the full bottle of wine and allow to simmer away until half the liquid is gone.

3 Cover with foil and pop into the oven at 160C/320F for at least three hours. Baste the ribs after two hours.

4 Bring them out and baste, then allow to rest for 15 to 20 minutes before serving with a sprinkling of fresh cut parsley. Use the leftover liquid as gravy.

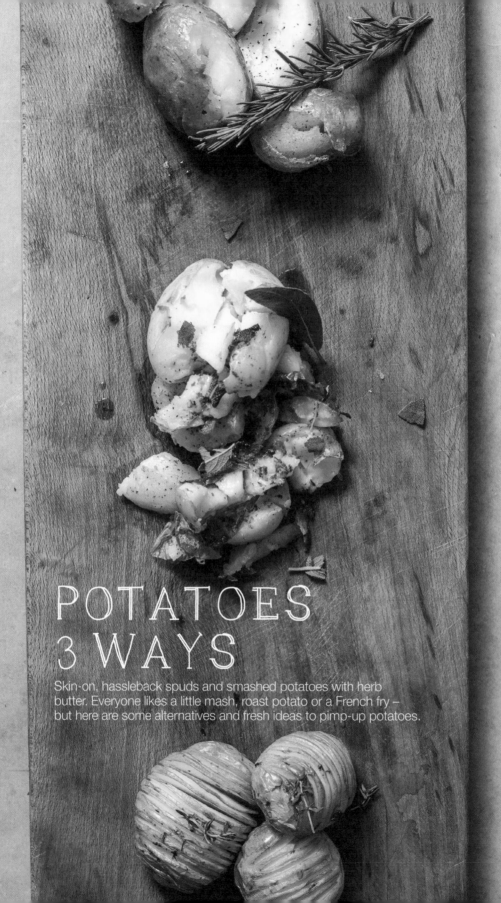

POTATOES
3 WAYS

Skin-on, hassleback spuds and smashed potatoes with herb
butter. Everyone likes a little mash, roast potato or a French fry –
but here are some alternatives and fresh ideas to pimp-up potatoes.

DEEP FRIED POTATOES WITH SKINS

SERVES 4

- 10 potatoes like roosters or russets, skin on and washed
- Salt
- 2 litres (½ gallon) oil for deep frying

1 Pop the potatoes into a pot of salted water and bring to the boil.
2 Cook the potatoes past the 'parboiled' stage but not completely done – al dente but with a hardness to the centre (basically slightly undercooked). Drain and allow to rest.
3 Heat a deep pot with oil until very hot (170C/340F). Drop a crumb of potato in; it must sizzle straight away.
4 Now onto the important stage.
5 Grab the potatoes and give each one a gentle squeeze to 'crack open' the skin. Lower them into the oil, trying not to break the potatoes.
6 Don't overcrowd the pot; this is best done in two stages.
7 Fry the potatoes for a few minutes until crispy and deep golden brown in colour. The skin should be nice and crispy.
8 Spoon out onto kitchen towel paper and sprinkle generously with salt.
9 Eat straight away.

HASSELBACK POTATOES

SERVES 4

- 8 medium potatoes/16 baby boil potatoes
- 1 clove garlic, thinly sliced
- 100g (½ cup) butter
- Splash of oil
- 1 teaspoon seasoning salt (like garlic, Cajun or celery salt)
- 1 teaspoon dried parsley/oregano
- Cracked black pepper

1 Preheat oven to 220C/430F
2 Grab each potato and slice all across the top in lines. Go quite deep but not all the way down, so the base is still intact as this holds all the slices together. A clever trick is to place each potato on a spoon and cut, as the spoon will prevent them from being cut all the way through.
3 Brush a baking tray with oil and place the potatoes in it, slices facing up.
4 In a separate bowl melt the butter and add the seasoning salt and dried herbs. Brush each potato generously with the butter. Slip a few slivers of garlic between the cuts to enhance the flavour.
5 Sprinkle generously with salt.
6 Bake the potatoes for around 40 to 50 minutes, until the outsides are nice and crispy and the insides are tender.
7 The slices should open up, which looks great on the plate.

SMASHED POTATOES

SERVES 4

- 8 medium potatoes/16 baby boil potatoes
- 150g (⅔ cups) butter
- 2 cloves garlic, grated
- Zest of 1 lemon
- Fresh sage and thyme
- Salt and pepper
- Preheat oven to 220C/430F.

1 Start by bringing the potatoes to the boil in salted water and cook.
2 When soft, drain and allow them to steam in the colander for about 5 minutes.
3 Meanwhile make up delicious garlic, lemon and sage flavoured butter by mixing the herbs together with the soft butter.
4 Line a baking tray with baking paper, put the potatoes on it and then lightly smash them with a masher. Gently break each potato, but allow them to still hold their shape a little.
5 Spoon little dollops of the butter over the potatoes. Add a sprinkle of salt and perhaps a few more herbs (brush herbs with oil first).
6 Bake for 25 minutes until golden. Serve with your favourite roast and a sharp sauce to cut the buttery goodness.
7 Top Tip: Experiment with different flavoured butters. Try black olive butter with anchovies; orange and sage butter; mustard and bacon, or – a personal favourite – sundried tomato and parsley.

BEAT THE
WINTER BLUES

Let's face it – here in Strandhill the winter can be a bit harsh. The limited daylight makes it a bit of a struggle to find time to get into the sea, and this takes a toll on everyone's fitness and motivation. But we try not to let ice, snow and wind stand in the way of a good time. Here are the tried-and-tested steps we revisit each winter to keep on top of the seasonal blues.

Go goal-oriented

If your sport is a competitive one, then the easiest way to get yourself in gear is to sign up for a challenge, such as your first 5k or an open-water swimming race. And if your main recreational activity isn't a competitive one – as in the case of surfing – then you can still apply the same tactic. Set yourself motivational goals like aiming to get in the water at least three times a week, or practical ones like getting all ten toes on that nose by springtime.

Psych yourself up

In the wintery surf world, absolutely nothing compares to a DVD of footage shot in warm, faraway waters. Focus on the moves you want to pull off and get them etched into your memory. Then on the day get amped with an appropriate soundtrack. Even if your main interest is a dry-land pursuit like rock climbing, never underestimate the power of a good mix. Some seriously cheesy, loud music can take you from wavering to fully committed in minutes.

A sprint, not a marathon

In the summer it's possible to surf for hours in relative comfort, but your body gets colder more quickly in winter, which obviously affects your ability to perform. Go for shorter sessions, but pack the action in. Don't hang about; go for the maximum number of waves you can and challenge yourself to get more moves in than you normally would. The same goes for any sport that's harder in chilly temps. If you're into jogging, get yourself out there, run for 10 minutes and mix in some sprints.

Get the right kit

You're hardly going to be motivated to take off on a rainy day bike ride if your waterproof is leaky and the dog ate your woolly hat. Similarly for surfers, there's no sense pretending you'll have a good time in a wetsuit with holes worn through the knees. If you've got the right gear, it will be that much easier to get yourself going. The days are shortest at the same time Christmas hits, so keep this in mind when formulating your wish list for Santa.

MAN V WAVES

To ride the world's biggest waves, it's nearly impossible for even the fittest person to paddle fast enough to catch them. But in tow-surfing, riders strap their feet into special boards designed to be pulled behind a jet-ski. The ski's job is to get the surfer up to the same speed as a wave that's about to break, at which point the surfer releases the tow rope and makes the drop into a **moving mountain of water.**

That's how our friend Barry Mottershead comes to regularly find himself inside truck-sized barrels at Ireland's premier big-wave breaks like Aileen's, Rileys and nearby Mullaghmore. Here he reveals what he puts in his stomach in order to pull it off.

"Generally with big wave surfing, I'm waking up before the crack of dawn in the dark. In tow-surfing, you've got triple the amount of work than a normal surf because you've got the whole boating element, the jet-ski and a massive long checklist of stuff to do. First thing I do is eat breakfast: Blackberries, porridge, natural yoghurt – get that down the hatch.

"When I'm out tow-surfing, it's always in the depths of winter. Just keeping the core warm is the main thing. I take a nice soup in a flask, wrap it up in a towel so it doesn't get smashed and stick it on the ski to drink between sessions out on the water. I love that. That's the thing I would cherish if I'm an old man thinking back – floating out in the wind with my Thermos, drinking soup.

"Afterwards, you're so wrecked by the time you get home in the dark. I nearly always go back to my girlfriend Liz's house. They're such a homely, lovely family, and they cook me a huge roast."

Barry Mottershead dwarfed by the wave at Mullaghmore

BIG PHAT VEGGIE NOODLE SOUP

Ahh yes the go-to meal on those days when the cold surf has done you in, when your body aches a little and your nose is full of seawater. The wind is howling outside, so put the TV on, grab your warmest socks, whip this up in 10 minutes and slurp away.

SERVES 2

- 1 packet ramen noodles
- 2 thumb-size pieces of ginger, finely sliced into sticks
- 3 cloves garlic, sliced
- 1 small onion, sliced
- ½ stick celery
- 1 red chilli (seeds in if you need to sweat it out), sliced
- 1 pepper, sliced (any colour)
- 2 scallions (green onions), sliced
- 1 portion veg, like broccoli, spinach, beans – preferably something green for health
- 50g (½ cup) coriander, chopped
- 2 tablespoons vegetable oil
- 1 tablespoon sesame oil
- 2 tablespoons soy sauce
- 750ml (3½ cups) veg stock (hot water from the kettle and organic veg cube)
- Coriander to garnish
- You need a wok

1. To begin, slice everything down nice and thin. Prep the work area and get organised because things are going to cook fast.
2. Put the kettle on as you need boiling water.
3. Grab the wok and heat it up with vegetable oil and sesame oil until it's just smoking.
4. Throw in the garlic for a few seconds, followed by the onions and ginger. Toss around the pan.
5. Next add in all the sliced veg (keep back half the scallion for garnishing). Stir fry as normal.
6. Add the hot stock or boiled water into the wok to create a 'quick' soup.
7. Throw in the ramen noodles (I usually add the packet of seasoning that comes with them).
8. Next a splash of light soy sauce.
9. Stir and cook through until noodles are soft.
10. Split between two bowls and garnish with scallions and coriander.
11. The secret here is all the flavour and goodness of the vegetables have been trapped in with the wok. Use plenty of ginger and garlic to combat the cold winter weather. To make more of a meal of this, add in cubed pieces of salmon or chicken pulled off the bone.

OK, SERIOUS MAC AND CHEESE!

A big favourite amongst my friends, perfect on a cold winter's night. There's a lot going on here so we'll break it up into four parts.

- Boil the macaroni and butternut squash
- Make a bacon and onion base
- Make a Béchamel cheese sauce
- Put it all together and bake it off

SERVES 6 TO 8

- 500g (5¼ cups) macaroni pasta
- 1 medium butternut squash
- 1 onion, diced
- 3 cloves garlic
- 200g (8oz) smoked bacon lardons
- 75g (2.5oz) air dried chorizo sausage, sliced into chunks
- 80g (½ cup) sundried tomatoes, chopped
- 1 teaspoon smoked paprika
- 1 teaspoon dried oregano
- Fresh sage brushed with oil
- Splash olive oil
- Salt and pepper

SAUCE

- 100g (½ cup) butter
- 80g (⅔ cup) flour
- 400ml (1¾ cups) milk
- 100ml (½ cup) white wine
- 100ml (½ cup) cream
- 2 tablespoons Dijon mustard
- 200g (¾ cup) grated vintage cheddar cheese
- Pinch white pepper
- ½ teaspoon grated nutmeg

FINALLY

- 200g (¾ cup) grated vintage cheddar cheese
- 1 tomato, sliced
- Sage (brushed with oil)

1 To start preheat the oven to 200C/395F.
2 Bring a large pot of well salted water to the boil and cook off the macaroni. Drain and rinse with cold water so it won't go starchy while you cook everything else.
3 Peel and chop the butternut to bite-size pieces and either roast, steam or boil the squash until soft and tender. Put to one side.
4 Grab a pan, add a splash of olive oil and fry off the onions, garlic and bacon. Later add the chorizo, smoked paprika and sundried tomatoes. Add some cracked black pepper. Once cooked, set side and sprinkle with oregano or sage.
5 In a separate, smaller pot on a low heat, melt the butter. Add the flour and stir hard with a wooden spoon to form a thick paste (also known as a roux). Add a splash of milk and stir, another splash of milk and stir. Change the wooden spoon to a whisk and slowly add all the milk, then the cream, continuously whisking up a nice smooth sauce. Keep stirring on a low heat.
6 Add in the wine, cheese, mustard, white pepper and a pinch of salt. Keep stirring until the cheese has melted through. If the sauce is getting too thick, add a splash of cold milk. The consistency should be like thick cream. If it's too thick it will make the dish way too stodgy.
7 Now grab a roasting dish; rub the inside with a clove of garlic and then smear on a layer of butter.
8 Pour in the macaroni and cooked butternut. Mix in the onion and bacon bits and stir together for an even mix of ingredients.
9 Pour on the cheesy, tangy sauce and spread over the rest of the ingredients. Cover the dish with the grated cheddar and top with thin slices of tomato.
10 Sprinkle with woody green herbs and pepper.
11 Bake for 25 minutes at 200C/395F.
12 Serve hot with a simple green salad and a Dijon mustard dressing. Bon appetit!

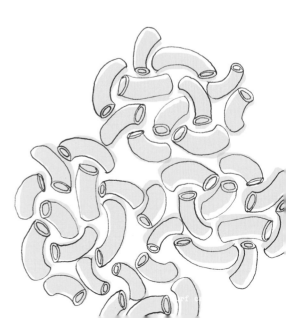

THE SHELLS CAFÉ CHICKPEA STEW

This big, hearty vegetable curry goes down well in the colder months at the café – so much so that we've been asked many times for the recipe. We just had to include it here, as it's lovely to serve on a cold winter's night. It tastes so good because there is a lot in it. Give it a go – vegetables can be substituted, so don't be afraid to use up whatever veg you have in the fridge like green beans, broccoli or cauliflower. Here goes...

SERVES 6 TO 8

- 2 tins chickpeas, drained
- 2 onions, diced
- 3 cloves garlic, diced
- 2 tablespoons ginger, grated
- 2 courgettes, cut into chunky slices
- 2 parsnips, peeled and cut into chunky slices
- 1 small butternut squash, peeled and cut into large chunks
- 1 red pepper, cut into large dices
- 1 green pepper, cut into large dices
- 2 chillies, diced
- 300g / 1 small bag baby spinach, split in two
- Handful fresh coriander
- 4 bananas
- 1 jar / 4 tablespoons plain yoghurt
- 1 tin coconut milk
- Butter
- Oil
- Spices: 2 teaspoons garam masala, 2 teaspoons cumin, 2 teaspoons turmeric, 3 teaspoons mild curry, 2 teaspoons fennel seed, 2 tablespoons sugar, and salt and pepper

1 Prepare the dish by peeling and dicing the veg, measuring the spices and having everything ready in front of you.

2 Grab a large heavy pot. Splash in 4 tablespoons of vegetable oil and let it get hot but not smoking hot. Toss in the garlic, wait a few seconds, then add the ginger, followed by the onions. Stir and sweat down a little until they begin to soften.

3 Scoop in all the dry herbs, then stir hard to flavour the oil and onions.

4 Next add all the veg (except the banana), half the spinach and the chickpeas. Stir everything around and throw in the butter to help cook and flavour the vegetables.

5 Once the vegetables start warming through add about 300ml (1½ cup) of water or vegetable stock; this helps steam and cook down the vegetables so they start to form a nice saucy texture.

6 Allow to simmer and cook down for about 30 minutes, perhaps adding some more water halfway though, if needed. This will depend on the water content of the vegetables.

7 You are looking for a nice, chunky, thick, soft stew with a deep yellow colour and exotic curry aroma. Fifteen minutes before the end add in a tin of coconut milk and most of the remaining spinach.

8 Stir and taste for seasoning, add salt and pepper or sugar and perhaps a dash of Tabasco if needed.

9 Serve hot in deep bowls; top the stew with fresh spinach, sliced banana and a dollop of yoghurt. The banana adds a sweetness and freshness to the dish.

MARK'S MIGHTY MONKFISH

Mark was the first real local we met when we moved to Strandhill. Myles and Mark are forever mulling over recipes, meals, tastes and flavours. It's great to surround yourself with people who love food as much as you do – it keeps you on your toes and helps you push the boundaries that little further with each dinner party. Mark makes a mean monkfish and it always wins us over when we go for dinner. As soon as we tasted it we knew it had to go in the book. Over to Mark...

This is my go-to, impress-a-girl dinner; it worked on my wife. Monkfish works for guys too as it's really meaty and substantial, like the pork chops of the sea. I prefer to have a little chilli with the fish to give it an edge, and you can't beat a lemon beurre blanc sauce – idiot-proof and tastes great. You can also change or add other ingredients, as it's delicious with any fish. The trick is just to add the butter slowly and whisk like hell! I normally serve this with lightly steamed asparagus or a side salad. Save room for dessert, which will hopefully be provided by the girl.

SAUCE
- 235ml (1 cup) dry white wine
- 1 large shallot, finely diced (about ⅓ cup)
- 55g (½ cup) cold butter, cut into small cubes (I use salted butter, but I tend not to add salt later on)
- 1 teaspoon white wine vinegar (I like tarragon white vinegar, but puritans will say this makes a Béarnaise sauce)
- 2 teaspoons fresh lemon juice, or more to taste

MAIN
- 50g (2½ tablespoons) sundried tomato pesto
- 1 small green chilli
- Handful fresh basil leaves
- Olive oil
- 4 x 200g (7oz) monkfish fillets
- 12 rashers (slices) Parma ham
- Salt and freshly ground black pepper

FOR THE SAUCE

1 Cook the wine, white wine vinegar and shallot in a small saucepan on a good heat, stirring occasionally, until the wine almost evaporates and the mixture looks glossy with no excess fluid. Remove the pan from the heat and whisk in the butter a couple of cubes at a time until melted and the sauce is thick and creamy (briefly return the pan to low heat if the butter is slow to melt). Off the heat, stir in the lemon juice and add salt and pepper to taste (personally, I don't think it needs any). Once you've made the sauce, to keep it warm just put it in a bowl and leave this in another bowl of warm water.

FOR THE FISH

1 Finely chop the chilli and basil, and mix with the pesto and a little olive oil; you can use a food processor to make a paste. (Freshly made pesto is much better, but most guys will run a mile from that!) I like to cover the monkfish in the paste for 30 minutes before cooking, but you don't need to if you're in a rush.

2 Oil a non-stick baking tray and place on it three slices of overlapping Parma ham. Spread with some of the paste, then place a monkfish fillet in the middle and wrap into a tight parcel. Repeat for each fillet then transfer to the fridge until needed. Some cocktail sticks are great for keeping it together. The fish should be fresh ideally, as frozen tends to be watery. I also like to put the parcels on a gas ring to sear the Parma before putting them in the oven, which makes the ham crispy.

3 When ready to cook, preheat the oven to 200C/400F. Sear in an oiled pan until each side is brown. Bake for 15 to 20 minutes, or until the ham is golden and the fish cooked through. Be careful, as monkfish can become tough if overcooked.

MAKE YOUR OWN BUTTER

SHAKE! SHAKE! SHAKE!

Making butter is a fun thing to do with kids, and our method doesn't require a churn – just a few pairs of helping hands!

Find a clean glass jar with a tight-fitting lid. Fill it one-third full with double cream. Now screw that lid on tight. Shake for three minutes – HARD. Pass it on to the next person, who needs to shake hard for three more minutes. By now you should see the cream starting to curdle. Keep passing the jar and shaking it up until a hard little butterball forms. Pour off the liquid residue, then plop the solid butter onto wax paper. Sprinkle this with sea salt, roll it into a sausage shape and refrigerate until the butter has hardened. And now there's nothing left to do but spread, snack and enjoy!

WOW

BUTTER FINGERS!

BRIOCHE

Our decadent, butter rich French loaf is a super delicious treat for breakfast. It looks challenging to make and it gets a bit messy, but the end result is so worth it.

   Makes two loaves (because one is never enough) and takes a whole day to make…

- 14g (4 teaspoons) dry yeast
- 50ml (¼ cup) warm water (not too warm)
- 600g (5 cups) 'strong' flour
- 75g (¾ cup) caster sugar
- 2 teaspoons salt
- 350g (1½ cups) butter, softened

1 Begin by getting the yeast working by mixing the water and yeast together. Allow it to work its magic for about five minutes.
2 Stir in the eggs and gently whisk. Mix the rest of the ingredients to form a tacky dough, and knead for a few minutes.
3 Spread the dough flat, then break the butter into small lumps and drop them on top.

GET READY TO GET MESSY!

4 Work all the butter into the dough, squeezing, pushing and pulling. Work it hard to get it all in until it forms a smooth and elastic texture.
5 Return to the bowl and allow to rest in a fridge until completely chilled. It can sit for a at least six hours and up to 48 hours in the fridge.
6 Line two loaf tins and divide the dough.
7 Lightly knead and shape the loaves to fit the tins and set aside for three to four hours.
8 As the dough warms up to room temperature the yeast will almost double the size of it.
9 Brush with a beaten egg and pop into a hot oven, at 180C/350F, for ten minutes. Then drop the temperature down to 160C/320F for a further 35 minutes.
10 Remove from the tins when still nice and hot; allow to cool on wire racks.
11 Enjoy with homemade jam and strong coffee. Or, like we do in Shells, make a brioche French toast by frying eggy brioche and serving with fruit, crème fraîche and a dusting of icing sugar.

B O W L
M E
O V E R

When it's cold and you crave cocoa, forego the mug. Serving hot chocolate French-style in a bowl feels like a little adventure and keeps hands warm too. Consider adding some cool ingredients like these favourites from Shells' supper club.

HOT HOT HOT!

Go South American with a tiny touch of chilli powder or cayenne pepper mixed into your cocoa. Just be careful not to overdo it! Garnish with a dollop of whipped cream and red sprinkles.

MERINGUE-GOO

As an alternative to marshmallows we often make unbaked meringues using egg whites and sugar. Pile it up on top and then finish off with a blowtorch if you've got one. Otherwise, dust with a grating of dark choc.

PULP ADDICTION

Whip Cointreau or another orange liqueur into heavy cream. Scoop this onto your hot chocolate, and follow up with fresh orange zest on top.

COLD COMFORT

In Italy, an affogato is made by pouring hot coffee over ice cream. Make an even richer version by mixing up thick hot chocolate in a jug – use about 3tsp extra cocoa per serving than you normally would. Serve each guest a cup holding a ball of ice cream, then let them pour hot chocolate on top.

COMPARE THE CARROT CAKE

Here are two recipes to try – compare and see which one becomes the favourite. Any excuse to bake and eat cake!

- 700g (3 cups) grated carrot
- 255g (2 cups) plain flour
- 3 teaspoons baking powder
- 1 teaspoon bicarbonate of soda
- 6 eggs
- 175g (¾ cup) dark soft sugar
- 80g (½ cup) caster sugar
- 400ml (1¾ cups) vegetable oil
- 100g (¾ cup) raisins
- 100g (¾ cup) walnuts
- ½ teaspoon cinnamon

CREAM CHEESE ICING

- 300g (1½ cups) cream cheese
- 150g (½ cup) butter, at room temperature
- 100g (½ cup) icing (powdered) sugar
- 1 teaspoon vanilla essence

1 Preheat oven to 180C/350F.

2 Begin with whisking together the sugar, oil and cinnamon. Throw in the eggs to make a nice sloppy mix.

3 Add in the sifted flour and baking powder, folding in the carrots, raisins, walnuts and bicarbonate of soda.

4 Pour the cake mix into two round springform cake tins (the average size is 25 to 30cm). Don't forget to butter or spray the cake tins to ensure they are non-stick.

5 Bake for around 40 minutes, or until a skewer comes out clean after inserting into the cake.

6 Turn them out onto wire racks and allow to cool.

7 To make the cream cheese icing beat the icing sugar and butter for a very long time – the longer the better. Then add in the cream cheese and vanilla essence and keep beating... Keep beating... You are looking for light and fluffy! Grab a dollop on your finger and take a good lick.

8 Next pick a beautiful plate, ice the cake in sandwich layers and dig in.

CARROT CAKE NO.2
FRUITY AND MOIST

This cake has banana in it, which helps keep it nice and moist.
It's my favourite carrot cake – thanks to Ruth for the recipe!

- 450g (4 cups) self-raising flour
- 300g (1½ cups) brown sugar
- 4 large eggs
- 2 teaspoons baking soda
- 3 to 4 large carrots, grated
- 100ml (½ cup) vegetable oil
- 100g (½ cup) raisins
- 100g (½ cup) walnuts, crushed
- ½ teaspoon ground cinnamon
- ½ teaspoon ground nutmeg
- 2 ripe bananas, mashed

ICING
- 100g (½ cup) butter, at room temperature
- 250g (1 cup) cream cheese
- 75g (¾ cup) icing sugar
- ½ teaspoon vanilla essence

Whisk together to form a great icing.

1 Preheat the oven to 180C/350F.

2 Beat the sugar and butter together.

3 While beating, add in the eggs, one at a time so as not to curdle the mix.

4 Next mix in the carrots, raisins, nuts, oil, cinnamon, nutmeg, baking soda and bananas. Mix them well and then fold in the flour to form a thick cake mix.

5 Pour into a lined cake tin and bake for 25 to 35 minutes. To test if the cake is cooked, poke a knife into the centre and ensure it does not have any raw cake mix on it when it comes out.

6 Allow to cool, turn out onto a wire cooling rack and scoop on the cream cheese icing.

7 Serve with a strong tea to a good group of friends.

BREW
THROUGH

Not so long ago coffee was seen as a bit of an indulgence, but increasingly in Ireland it is becoming an essential. Loads of customers in Shells want advice on making coffee at home. Whatever method you choose, it's a lovely process to make it and a nice break to your day.

French press or cafetière

Pros: Requires only one piece of equipment with two simple parts; can make one pot for a whole crowd
Cons: Getting the coffee grounds out of the carafe is never as easy as you want it to be; pot tends to go cold quite quickly

Drip filter baskets

Pros: Quite trendy; methodical preparation so you can make this into a bit of a ritual; needs only one very small piece of kit
Cons: Takes a while, because you have to pour a bit, then wait, pour, wait and so on

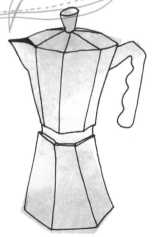

Coffee machine

Pros: Makes enough for several servings with hardly any effort
Cons: Requires electricity, space on the countertop and a supply of filters; the thin glass carafes have a habit of breaking easily

Espresso machine

Pros: You can make a variety of different drinks; it's the real deal and packs a punch
Cons: Makes only one cup at a time; requires more technique and space than other methods

Aero-Press espresso maker

Pros: Produces espresso through a vacuum action rather than a machine so you get a little workout; quite compact to store
Cons: An Aero-Press comprises several parts, so it's not the easiest cleanup

Moka espresso maker

Pros: Can make espresso on a single cooking ring – you don't even need a kettle; good option for a campervan
Cons: Time consuming; has to be watched closely

Myles' camel-man way to make campfire coffee
In perfecting this bushwhacker method, it helps to have a wild beard, raggedy hat, dirty t-shirt, shredded shorts and dusty boots. Perfected during his years as a safari guide, Myles insists it drives the ladies wild.

- Get hot water on the go in your campfire kettle.
- Pour fresh ground coffee right into the pot.
- Throw in some broken eggshells... and don't worry – it's going to get even weirder.
- Let your coffee brew.
- Put a long stick into the fire so that the end catches fire and becomes covered in hot ash.
- Plunge the glowing stick into the pot and give a good stir.
- The ash will combine with the coffee grounds and collect on the bottom, and the eggshells will trap them there.
- Slowly serve into cups; with practice, you should get a pretty clean pour.

BURIED TREASURE

Salvage yards are an incredible source of inspiration. They can of course be a bit daunting – you'll rarely encounter a price tag and will have to get used to trawling through draughty sheds. But the payoff is absolutely worth it. So follow these tips, get your hands dirty and score some gorgeous one-off bargains.

OUR FAVOURITE SALVAGE YARD FINDS

- Old mirrors
- Ladders – these make great towel racks
- Timber for cabinet cladding, bedroom flooring and feature walls
- The bathroom sink and tap
- Scaffolding planks to use as shelves, benches and raised garden beds

- Your first step is to research opening times and locations. Some yards have websites and many do not, so be prepared to pick up the phone and do your homework. Discover each firm's speciality too – for example ironwork, timber, industrial fittings and so forth.

- Find out which businesses accept cards and which are cash only, then remember to fill your wallet accordingly.

- Know your style. For example, we wanted an industrial-style cottage look. Having a brief in mind will help you to focus as you browse.

- Dress appropriately so that you can focus, take your time and be comfortable. Stuff is often outside on pallets so be ready for the elements, from scorching sun to pouring rain.

- Spread your reach. Instead of sticking close to home, get in the car and go on an adventure. The further you travel, the more variety of merchandise you'll encounter.

- Introduce yourself at the office. The person behind the desk is a goldmine of knowledge, someone who can keep an eye out for what you're looking for, direct you to relevant resources and share ideas on anything from application to installation.

- Bring pictures, for example snapshots and magazine clippings, so that you can easily communicate what you're looking for or hoping to achieve.

- You'll get home and want to follow up, so be sure to pick up business cards and mobile numbers.

- Ultimately people want to sell their stock, so ask for help and don't be shy.

- Find out about delivery. It's all well and good if you love that church pew, but if you can't lug it home and the yard can't deliver it to you, then you might have to let it go.

- If you're passing by outside of opening hours, call the office anyway because plenty of places will open up if a customer is waiting at the gate.

- Some things will need to be repaired, so speak to the salvage yard staff and get contact details for their recommended experts. And don't be daunted! A cast iron bath with chipped enamel can be fixed, and still might come in cheaper than a new one – and you'll have a unique piece that you really love.

- Be brazen – it's all about the bargain! There are no fixed prices in most yards, so it's a matter of striking a deal. Have a price limit so you don't go mad in the heat of the moment, and use Google on your phone to compare prices with the going rate.

- If you love something for whatever reason, buy it there and then. Particularly when it's a one-off; if you hesitate it will be gone!

GET CRAFTY

CREATE AN ENVELOPE-BACKED PILLOW COVER WITH FASHION AND HANDBAG DESIGNER ANA FAYE

I fell in love with Ana Faye's bags, and asked her design some cushions for our home. Here she shows us how to make one of her fabulous pillow covers...

Ana says: Before I unleash you into this tutorial there are a few tips I want to share that I've always found useful:

Use something like a coffee sack, tablecloth or old blankets – basically heavier fabric if you can. It not only stands up to more knocks than cotton fabric, but it also gives the pillow a better shape. Be a bit of a miser when it comes to cutting your fabric. A snug fitting pillowcase makes for a plumper pillow.

Tools and Materials:
- Basic sewing supplies
- Pillow insert
- Fabric
- Velcro, cut to the length of the pillow

Instructions:

Step 1
- Measure the dimensions of your pillow. To determine the size and shape of fabric you'll need, add 1 inch (2.5cm) to the height and length, then add ½ inch (1.5cm) for the seam allowance.
- For example, for a pillow measuring 20 inches square, add on 1.5 inches, so we'll mark one square out on the fabric fabric measuring 21.5 inches (54cm) square. This will be the front of the pillow, marked "A". With a disappearing ink fabric pen or tailors' chalk and a ruler, draw the dimensions of this piece onto your fabric.
- Now you need two pieces for the envelope part at the back of the pillow. Decide how far down you want the opening to be. Let's just say 6 inches (15cm); now mark your 21.5 inches (54cm) width across the fabric with chalk, then come down 6 inches and add another 3 inches (7.5cm) onto it. This will be where the fabric folds under and where the Velcro will sit. So the rectangle will be 21.5 inches (54cm) in width and 9 inches (23cm) in length. With a disappearing ink fabric pen or tailors' chalk and a ruler, draw the dimensions of piece "B" onto your fabric.
- The top piece is now 6 inches plus the extra 3 inches for the fold, so that's 21.5 inches minus 6 inches, which equals 15.5 inches (40cm). So we know to cut piece "C" 21.5 inches across in width and 15.5 inches plus 3 inches (for the fold down), which comes to 18.5 inches (47cm). With a disappearing ink fabric pen or tailors' chalk and a ruler, draw the dimensions of piece "C" on the fabric.
- Zigzag stitch all the edges to stop the fabric from fraying.
- Note: If you wish to line your pillow as we did with this coffee sack, cut all the above in the same measurements in lining fabric.

Step 2
- Iron down the fabric along the fold line 3 inches (15cm) from the top on the two back pieces.
- Sew on the Velcro on to both sides of the now ironed fold at the back, 1 inch (2.5cm) in from the edge of the fold line.

Step 3
- Now line up the two backs so the Velcro closes and you should have two back pieces that join together to make one square the same measurement as the front piece "A".

Step 4
- Pin any trim to the right side of the fabric (like bobbles, piping, lace – anything you like really) ¼ inch (6mm) in from the edge of the front part of the piece "A". Now run a stitch over them to hold them in place.

Step 5
- Take the two back pieces that are stuck together with Velcro and pin the right sides of the fabric together in place the whole way around; sew with a ½-inch (13mm) seam allowance all around your pillow's edges.

Step 6
- Trim off the corners to get nice clean edges.

Step 7
- Turn the pillow cover right side out. Use a point turner or a closed pair of scissors to push the corners out. Stuff in the pillow insert.

Step 8
- Now lounge and have a nice cup of coffee!
- Have fun,

AN OUTSIDE-OF-THE-BOX CHRISTMAS

Christmas is one of the only times in the year we get to spend the whole day with our family, so we really push the boat out with our festive spread. Since the average person ends up facing the exact same menu for every festive occasion, by December 25th we're sick of eating traditional Christmas dinner! Most of us have already had our fill of boring turkey and roast potatoes, so in an attempt to think outside-the-box, here's our alternative Christmas menu to serve up on the big day.

Meat – Christmas is already an expensive enterprise, so treat your bank account kindly by being savvy with meat choices. Cuts suited to braising tend to be cheap and provide real wow factor when feeding a crowd.

Sauces – You can break beyond traditional gravy by introducing more interesting sauces, especially anything incorporating seasonal flavours – think mace, juniper berries, cloves, nutmeg, dark spices and even chocolate.

Sides – Couscous is dead easy, quick and cheap. Use it as a base for seasonal ingredients – just chuck in dried fruits, nuts, orange zest, dried cranberries and the like.

Veg – Even though we're in Ireland, we're not afraid of deviating from the traditional potato path. This time of year we love to serve sweet potatoes and parsnips roasted with a drizzle of honey.

Drinks – Mulled wine is all well and good, but even hardcore fans will appreciate a break midway into December. Instead heat up apple juice and draw out a new dimension by adding ginger or lacing it with calvados or try making eggnog, spiced pear juice or pomegranet cocktails.

Salad – We're all craving a healthy choice in this season of indulgence, so add festive dazzle to a salad with fresh red currants, green pistachios and ruby-red pomegranate seeds.

Dessert – Mince pies are a holiday perennial, but we like to give them a new twist with a fantastic topping. Just soften a bit of vanilla ice cream and mix in alcohol soaked prunes.

ALTERNATIVE XMAS TREE

I love different colours and textures of paper and tapes, and use any excuse to collect them. So I came up with a creative and fun tree which is pretty much hassle free. Even if you do have a real tree, this is a great way to make the kids' room, or any other room, feel festive.

Here's how:
- Cut varying lengths of different coloured paper.
- Gather a selection of paper tapes (these are great, as they have the same sticking power as masking tape, but won't leave marks on the walls or pull off paintwork).
- Stack the paper in even lines to form the shape of a Christmas tree.
- If you have any scraps of wool or cards (or other colourful bits and bobs), you can layer these on too.
- Have fun, and remember nothing is permanent so you can try as many colours and designs as you like.
- Ho, ho, ho!

FESTIVE FRUITY MINCE PIES

There's more than one way to get fruity at Christmas. Give these mince pies a try, they're ridiculously easy to make and they're so much nicer than shop bought ones.

THE MINCEMEAT

- 225g (2 cups) Bramley apples, cored and chopped small
- 110g (½ cup) shredded suet
- 175g (1 cup) raisins
- 110g (½ cup) sultanas
- 110g (½ cup) dried cranberries
- 110g (½ cup) mixed peel, chopped
- 175g (¾ cup) soft dark brown sugar
- Grated zest and juice of 1 orange
- Grated zest and juice of 1 lemon
- 25g (¼ cup) almonds, slivered
- 2 level teaspoons mixed ground spice
- ¼ level teaspoon ground cinnamon
- Good pinch freshly grated nutmeg
- 4 to 5 tablespoons brandy, rum or whiskey

1 Simply combine all of the ingredients except the alcohol in a large bowl and mix thoroughly.
2 Cover the bowl with a clean cloth and leave in a cool place overnight or for 12 hours, for the flavours to develop and mingle.
3 Preheat the oven to 120C/225F.
4 Cover the ovenproof container loosely with foil and place it in the oven for three hours, then remove the container from the oven. Don't worry about the appearance of the mincemeat, which will look like it is swimming in fat. This is how it should look.
5 As it cools, stir it from time to time; the fat will coagulate and, instead of it being in shreds, it will encase all the other ingredients.
6 When the mincemeat is quite cold, stir in the alcohol and pack in sterilised jars. The mincemeat will keep for ages in a cool, dark cupboard but I think it's best eaten within a year!

THE PIES

MAKES 16 TO 18 PIES

- 225g (1 cup) butter, cubed
- 350g (2½ cups) plain flour
- 100g (½ cup) golden caster sugar
- 280g (1½ cups) homemade mincemeat
- 1 small egg
- Icing sugar to dust

1 To make the pastry, rub the butter into the flour, then mix in the caster sugar. This stage can be made easier by putting all ingredients into a food processor.

2 Combine the pastry into a ball – don't add any liquid and knead briefly.

3 The dough will be fairly firm, like a shortbread dough. You can use the dough immediately, chill or freeze it.

4 Preheat the oven to 200C/350F. Line 18 holes of two 12-hole patty tins, by pressing small walnut-sized balls of pastry into each hole. Spoon the mincemeat into the pies.

5 Take slightly smaller balls of pastry than before and pat them out between your hands to make round lids. Top the pies with their lids, pressing to seal the edges – you won't need milk or egg to seal them as they will stick on their own.

6 Beat a small egg and brush the tops of the pies. Bake for 20 minutes or until golden. Leave to cool slightly in the tin before removing to a wire rack. To serve, lightly dust with icing sugar. They will keep for three to four days in an airtight container, but once you try one they'll be lucky to last the day!

THE DROP IN

Oh no, some friends have dropped by for a glass of wine and not tea and biscuits! Here are some quick and easy snacks to impress.

SPICED NUTS

- 3 handfuls of different nuts, like whole almonds, shelled pistachios, brazil nuts, peanuts
- 1 teaspoon mixed spice
- 1 teaspoon cumin
- Pinch cracked black pepper
- Salt
- Paprika, cayenne, sesame seeds, coriander seeds (optional)

1 Grab a big heavy pan and put it on full heat. Throw in all the herbs and spices and gently toast them. Next stir in the nuts and warm them through. The spices will infuse the nuts.

2 Allow to rest for a minute and serve. The spiced nuts will keep for ages in a sealed container. Just warm them up again next time!

HOMEMADE TORTILLA CHIPS

1 Grab your lunch wraps or tortilla wraps, roll them up and cut into strips.

2 Drop them into a pot of hot oil (175C/350C) and deep fry them for 20 seconds.

3 Scoop them out onto a paper towel to cool and go crispy. Toss them into a bowl, sprinkle generously with salt and Cajun spice.

4 Homemade chips!

(GOES DOWN REALLY WELL WITH OUR SESAME DIP ON PAGE 176)

BAKED CAMEMBERT

This seems really fancy but it's so easy and quick to make.

- 1 Camembert
- 1 clove garlic
- Rosemary
- Crusty bread
- Good wine

1 Preheat the oven to 180C/350F.

2 Grab the round of soft cheese and make a foil basket to hold the cheese in. Poke a few holes into the cheese with a knife and shove a few slivers of garlic into the cheese. Next add the rosemary sticks. Bake the cheese for around 10 to 15 minutes, until soft and gooey and you get that stinky cheese smell.

3 Place onto a chopping board and tuck in with large pieces of chunky, fresh, crusty bread.

4 This is delicious!·

5 It's also a good ice breaker as everyone has to get up close to get stuck into the cheese. As my friend Mark says, it's stretch or starve!

BREAD DIP: EGYPTIAN DUKKAH

This nutty dip is traditionally served by dipping crusty bread into olive oil and then into the dukkah. It packs a lot of flavour and has so many uses. We make up batches in Shells and sell it in our Little Shop next door – it is one of those products that we just can't make enough of. Once you get onto it, it becomes addictive!

This is a great way to start a meal – the simple touch of breaking bread together. We place the bread on our central island and everyone just gathers around, chatting and nibbling and dipping! It's less formal than seating people straight away and creates a relaxed vibe. Plus it frees you up to work away on the main course while everyone is settling.

Make sure you have a super-good quality olive oil. I love one with notes of grass and greenness to really complement the bread. Be generous with the portion too.

SERVES AROUND 6

- 200g (1½ cups) hazlenuts
- 160g (1 cup) sesame seeds
- 3 tablespoons coriander seeds
- 3 tablespoons cumin seeds
- 1 tablespoon fennel seeds
- 1 tablespoon cracked black pepper
- 2 pinches salt
- 1 pinch chilli flakes
- Extra virgin olive oil and crusty bread to serve

1 Begin by toasting the hazlenuts for 10 minutes at 180C/350F. Allow to cool and remove the skin by rubbing them in a clean tea towel.
2 Heat a large frying pan and toss in the sesame seeds and spices. Toast them all lightly until they begin to pop. Stir frequently.
3 Place all the ingredients into a food processor and blitz gently until they are coarsely chopped. Alternatively you can do this by hand with a pestle and mortar.
4 Season with salt and serve.

PERIWINKLES

These are a great snack and always get everyone talking. There is a bit of a knack to extracting the cooked winkles out of their shells, but a great little morsel awaits the eager! This is sure to evoke horror from some and smiles from others.

Pop the winkles into a pot of boiling water – three to four minutes should do the trick. Drain and allow to cool a little. Start picking away by twisting out the meat with a thick needle or toothpick. Nibble away. For extra flavour dip into a herby mayo or batter with breadcrumbs. Your friends will be talking about this experience for a few days to come.

THE
BIT
AT
THE
BACK

MYLES' TIPS FOR COOKING AT HOME

My first rule is: start simple and don't try to over-achieve with something from a restaurant or the TV. Understand the basics of frying, boiling and baking and what needs high action heat or low and slow cooking. It sounds straightforward but you'd be surprised how many people get these simple things wrong. To get it right follow these basic rules:

- Steak needs high heat whereas fish would only require medium heat. The more delicate the item the more careful the cooking and temperature need to be.

- Always take recipes with a pinch of salt. Read them beforehand and make any changes to suit your taste, ingredients and so on.

- Good ingredients are probably the most important, especially when cooking simple dishes. Good ingredients will give you confidence in cooking; cheap bacon just can't compete with a locally smoked pancetta. This is where your local market and butcher come into play. Food from giant supermarkets is so mass-produced that the flavour just isn't there. Stick to small artisan suppliers.

- It's always great to start to grow your own, even start with your fave vegetable and salads. You'll notice the flavour difference and the freshness.

USEFUL CONVERSION TABLES

OVEN TEMPERATURE CONVERSIONS

Farenheit	Centigrade	Gas Mark	Description
225 F	110 C	¼	Very Cool
250 F	130 C	½	
275 F	140 C	1	Cool
300 F	150 C	2	
325 F	170 C	3	Very Moderate
350 F	180 C	4	Moderate
375 F	190 C	5	
400 F	200 C	6	Moderately Hot
425 F	220 C	7	Hot
450 F	230 C	8	
475 F	240 C	9	Very Hot

US LIQUID MEASUREMENTS

1 gallon	4 quarts	3.79 L (can round to 4L)
1 quart	2 pints	.95 L (can round to 1L)
1 pint	2 cups	16 fl. oz. or 450 ml
1 cup	8 fl oz	225 ml (can round to 250ml)
1 tablespoon (Tbsp.)	½ fl oz	16 ml (can round to 15 ml)
1 teaspoon (tsp.)	⅓ tablespoon	5 ml

BRITISH LIQUID MEASUREMENTS

1 UK pint	0.56 ltrs	
1 UK liquid oz	0.96 US liquid oz	
1 pint	570 ml	16 fl oz
1 breakfast cup	10 fl oz	½ pint
1 tea cup	⅓ pint	
1 Tablespoon	15 ml	
1 dessert spoon	10 ml	
1 teaspoon	5 ml	⅓ Tablespoon
1 ounce	28.4 g	can round to 25 or 30
1 pound	454 g	
1 kg	2.2 pounds	

INTERNATIONAL LIQUID MEASUREMENTS

Country	Standard Cup	Standard Teaspoon	Standard Tablespoon
Canada	250 ml	5 ml	15 ml
Australia	250 ml	5 ml	20 ml
UK	250 ml	5 ml	15 ml
New Zealand	250 ml	5 ml	15 ml

MUST-HAVE
KITCHEN
ESSENTIALS...

Salt

When it comes to basic seasoning, don't have just one type of salt. The choice is incredible, from smoked salts to flavoured salts to pink salts. It's the same with pepper: this is a great way to experiment and add colour and flavour to your dish.

Spices and herbs

As for the rest of the spice box, include smoked paprika, ground herbs and whole herbs. You should always have a selection. When using dry herbs, use them in the initial part of cooking, cook them through and then add the ingredients. This imparts a better flavour. (Unless it's dried chilli.) Leave fresh herbs to the end. If you're baking with fresh herbs, brush them with olive oil first, as this makes them go crispy instead of drying out

Oils and vinegars

I have at least seven or eight different oils on the go at any time. Whenever we go away, we bring home a new flavour. It's a great item you can really use. Start a collection. I think it's good to have about six oils and four vinegars to choose from. The differences in flavour can really give you confidence in your cooking. Experiment by infusing your oils and vinegars with herbs, too.

Oils:
- Olive oil for basic cooking
- Groundnut oil for high heat cooking
- Sesame oil for Asian flavour
- Infused oils to add depth, like mushroom
- Nut oils are great in salad dressings

Vinegars:
- White wine for buttery, creamy sauces
- Cider vinegar for chutneys and preserving
- Red wine vinegar for meats and braising, and generally deeper flavour in cooking
- Balsamic vinegar for delicate, sharp, sweet flavours in salads or with fruits
- Sherry vinegar, for egg dishes
- Rice vinegar in Asian dishes
- Tarragon vinegar for sauces, especially hollandaise

Condiments

These can be fun. Get your travelling friends to bring you something interesting back from overseas. The basics to have are chutneys, mayos, mustards and relishes. We have six types of mustard – wholegrain, Dijon, English, hot horseradish, wasabi and French. And that's just mustard…

Stocks and sauces

Skip the usual big brands and look for some fantastic organic stocks in your local health food store or artisan food shop. They have fewer preservatives and a lot more flavour. Look out for free-range chicken stock, too. Bovril is always good to have as part of your stock collection. And I know we all hate being prepared, but if you make a good stock, freeze it into cubes for future use. After you do this once, you really will thank yourself.

Tools

The best tool to invest in is a decent, sharp knife. Visit your butcher to get your knives sharpened. When you're selecting pans, the rule of thumb is the heavier the better as they spread and hold the heat more evenly. A couple of casserole dishes are great. We got a fantastic one from Jane's mum, which is over 30 years old and still going strong. A few baking trays are always handy, too. Real wood chopping boards are great. We sell a fantastic range in our little shop, all hand carved, and thick, solid pieces.

I like to have a microplane – it's like a long grater and a proper zester. I can't live without mine. I even brought one all the way to my aunt's bakery business in the Caribbean – that's how important I think they are! You'll use it a lot more than you think. Another tool I love is a mandolin, for the perfect slice each time. The Japanese brands tend to be very good. It will provide you with great salads and prepped veg. Just watch your fingertips!

LISTINGS

If you're visiting the local area, here's some information on activities to do in the area, local producers and where to eat, sleep and drink. As we've said before many a time, this beautiful corner of Ireland will enchant you so come and visit soon, it will set you free!

ACCOMMODATION

Clarion Hotel Sligo

Located on the outskirts of Sligo town and overlooked by the majestic Benbulben Mountain is the four-star Clarion Hotel Sligo, which dates back to 1848 and was designed by William Dean Butler. Facilities include; 162 bedrooms including 89 suites, Sinergie Restaurant, Kudos Bar & Restaurant, SanoVitae Health & Leisure Club, Essence Spa, two converted churches on site.

Address: Clarion Hotel, Clarion Road, Co. Sligo.
Tel: (353) 71 911 9000
Email: info@clarionhotelsligo.com
Web: www.clarionhotelsligo.com

Cois Re Holiday Apartments

We offer 4 star Bord Failte approved luxury self catering accommodation in the heart of Yeats Country. These luxury self-catering holiday apartments are spacious and modern. Cois Ré is ideally situated for golf enthusiasts and surfers alike, being just a short walk to the beach and local golf course. We are also within easy walking distance of an array of bars, restaurants and other amenities.

Address: Cois Re Holiday Apartments, Strandhill, Co. Sligo.
Tel: (353) 87 957 4358
Email: carmel@coisreapartments.com
Web: www.coisreapartments.com

Cromleach Lodge 4 Star Country House Hotel & Ciúnas Spa

Just 5 minutes off the N4 at Castlebaldwin, Cromleach Lodge overlooks Lough Arrow and the Bricklieve Mountains. Facilities include; 57 Bedrooms, most with views of Lough Arrow, Moira's Award Winning Restaurant, Nuadas Bar, De Dannan Lounge & Ciúnas Spa.

Address: Lough Arrow, Castlebaldwin, Co. Sligo.
Tel: (353) 71 916 5155
Email: info@cromleach.com
Web: www.cromleach.com

Seashore B&B

Seashore is an Award-Winning Country Home situated on a three-acre site, offering Luxury Accommodation. We are 8km from Strandhill and just 50 metres from the sea. Enjoy breakfast in the conservatory/dining room overlooking Knocknarea, the Ox Mountains and Ballysadare Bay.

Address: Off Ballina Road, Lisduff, Ballysadare, Co.Sligo.
Tel/Fax: (353) 71 916 7827
Email: seashore@oceanfree.net
Web: www.seashoreguests.com

The Strandhill Lodge and Suites

The Strandhill Lodge and Suites is a four-star Luxury Boutique Hotel in Strandhill. Voted Best Small Hotel in Ireland 2013. This 21 room guesthouse in the shadow of Knocknarea comprises 18 deluxe rooms and three suites, with a mix of rooms with balconies, patios and superior two-room suites. Located 2 mins from Shells Café, Strandhill.

Address: Strandhill Lodge and Suites, Top Road, Strandhill, Co. Sligo.
Tel: (353) 71 912 2122
Email: info@strandhilllodgeandsuites.com
Web: strandhilllodgeandsuites.com

EATING OUT

Coach Lane

Multi-Award winning restaurant Coach Lane @ Donaghys is one of the longest standing and most highly regarded dining establishments in Sligo. Boasting a nationwide reputation for excellent food, warm, professional service and comfort beyond compare, no visit to Sligo is complete without the Coach Lane experience.

Address: 1 Lord Edward St, Co. Sligo.
Tel: (353) 71 916 2417
Email: coachlanesligo@gmail.com

Kates Kitchen

Independent fine foods & toiletry store with delicious homemade lunches and treats to takeaway. Open Monday to Saturday. Do call!

Address: Kates Kitchen, 3 Castle Street, Co. Sligo.
Tel: (353) 71 914 3022
Email: info@kateskitchen.ie
Web: www.kateskitchen.ie

Mammy Johnston Ice Cream Parlor

Local coffee shop and ice cream parlor, established by Mammy Johnston in the 40s. Mummy Johnson's secret hand made ice cream recipe has been passed down to her grandsons, who make it onsite using locally sourced fresh ingredients.

Address: The Sea Front, Strandhill, Co. Sligo.

Tra Ban Restaurant

Located in Strandhill above the Strand Bar, Tra Bhán Restaurant is rapidly establishing itself as a must-stop culinary destination of the North West. Specialising in fresh, local produce, Tra Bhán's mouth watering menu comprises of meat, seafood and vegetarian options.

Address: Above The 'Strand Bar', Strandhill, Co. Sligo.
Tel: (353) 71 912 8402
Email: trabanstrandhill@gmail.com

LISTINGS

RETAILERS
Sheerins Meatin Place Ballymote
Bringing his world wide travels to the butcher shop Adrian Sheerin is now the 'All Ireland Supreme Sausage Champion'. From traditional sausage to chorizo, they are all hand made on the premises in Ballymote using locally sourced ingredients.
Address: Teeling Street, Ballymote, Co. Sligo.
Tel: (353) 71 918 3671

PUBS AND NIGHTCLUBS
The Strand Bar
The Strand Bar is run by three former Irish surf team members and is famous for its live music and good food.
Address: The Strand Bar & Restaurant, Shore Road, Strandhill, Co. Sligo.
Tel: (353) 91 716 8140
Web: www.thestrandbar.com
facebook.com/thestrandbar
twitter.com/thestrandbar

Velvet Room Nightclub
Opens Saturdays and Bank Holiday Sundays from 11.30pm til Late. Over 21s only.
Address: Velvet Room, Kempton Promenade, Sligo Town
Tel: Table Reservations - (353) 71 914 4721
Email: info@velvetroom.ie
Web: www.velvetroom.ie

ACTIVITY CENTERS
Seatrails
Seatrails provides guided archaeological walking tours within the beautiful Strandhill and Knocknarea peninsula which has a fascinating past with many interesting heritage sites to see. Your guide is a professional maritime archaeologist and a Wild Atlantic Way ambassador for Sligo.
Web: www.seatrails.ie

Standhill National School
Strandhill National School is located on an idyllic two acre site, overlooking the golf course and sea. All the local amenities and the wider community feature in the holistic education of the pupils.
Address: Strandhill, Co. Sligo.
Tel: (353) 71 916 8154
Email: asicus81@gmail.com
Web: www.strandhillnationalschool.ie

Strandhill Surf School
Strandhill Surf School is the centre of surfing in Strandhill, Sligo.We have a great location in a corner premises on the beachfront. Run by owner Paul Buchanan,from New Zealand, it is a great place to learn to surf or improve your surfing skills.
Address: Beach Front, Strandhill, Co. Sligo.
Tel: (353) 71 9168483
Email: strandhillsurfschool@gmail.com
Web: www.strandhillsurfschool.com

ATTRACTIONS
VOYA Seaweed Baths
Imagine relaxing back into a luxurious steaming bath of fresh seawater and wild, organic seaweed. Our VOYA Seaweed Baths and organic treatments are especially recommended for those who are over worked, stressed or simply seeking an effective natural detoxifying process for the skin. VOYA Seaweed baths will delight and relax.
Address: Voya Seaweed Baths, Strandhill, Co. Sligo.
Tel: (353) 71 916 8686
Email: info@voyaseaweedbaths.com
Web: www.voyaseaweedbaths.com

Waxon Surfboards
Ireland's Waxon Surfboards design and shape custom surfboards. Conor and the Waxon team work with you to design, shape and create a surfboard to your individual specifications.
Address: Waxon Surfboards, Benbulben Craft Centre, Rathcormac, Co. Sligo.
Tel: (353) 86 821 2418
Email: waxonsurfboards@ireland.com
Web: www.waxonsurfboards.ie

NOTES...

INDEX

THANKS!

We are so grateful to have the chance to share our experience and also to document the process of creating our beach house.

Massive thanks to Jon Wiggins (architect) and Derek Shaw and his team of builders for helping us realise our dream home. For sticking with us, when we brought home the most random of items to be installed in the house and for believing in our vision.

A super big thanks to Paula Mills of Sweet William Illustrations (www.lovelysweetwilliam.blogspot. com) for the amazing illustrations and input to the book. Paula adds the colour and beauty to the pages as only she can.

Shannon Denny (writer) and Mike Searle (photographer) for the jam packed week of photos, story telling and of course eating the plates and plates of gorgeous food! What a week and an experience to share.

There are so many people who contributed time, ideas, skills, recipes and love to this book... here you are in no particular order... Mark Capilitan, Andrew Kilfeather, Sarah Elvey, Julien Vial, Shelley Gardner, Gary Smith, Mary, Leonie, Mark, Andrea Flanagan, Annette, Kealin and Harry Noone.

To Louise, David and all the gang at Orca Publications for the vision and energy to keep the project moving and of course to pull it all together and make it look and feel so good!

Big thanks to all the Shells Café & Little Shop crew who held everything together while we were so absorbed in this. To Julien and Sarah from Shells for sharing their favourite recipes.

And of course the big thanks is to you, the reader, for supporting us and for buying this book. We wouldn't be here without the support of all of our loyal Shells fans and Surf Café book fans. It's an amazing journey and we are so glad you have jumped on board with us

Jane & Myles